4th July 2024

TALES OF TH[...]

MEMOIRS OF AN
EAST END GUTTERSNIPE

*For Dad,
with greatest affection,
Paul.*

BRIAN WALKER

© Brian Walker 2016

The right of Brian Walker to be identified as the author of this work has been asserted by him in accordance with the Copyright, Design and Patents Act 1988

Illustrations by Brian Walker

Book design by Laurence Payne

First edition 2016

This KDP edition 2020

With great affection I dedicate this book to my dad, Sid Walker.

INTRODUCTION
Tales of the Old Iron Pot

This mysterious phrase has been used in our family for generations, I'm not sure of its origins and any attempts to find out have been unsuccessful.

It was certainly used to describe my old man's long winded and detailed stories of when he was a boy and of the many characters who he knew when he lived with his large family on the banks of the River Lea at Lea Bridge. Whenever we had visitors he was in his element telling these colourful tales with vigour and lots of hand movements. I have no doubt that it was him that gave me my love of stories and the ability to talk for hours.

ACKNOWLEDGEMENTS

Many thanks to that small band of friends who have aided and encouraged me in the production of this book.

Firstly, the maestro, Tony Locantro. From the start Tony has believed in me and my ability. His constant encouragement has been an inspiration to me and he has provided considerable aid in the apostrophe department.

Thanks to my wife for putting up with my silent periods when an idea slipped into my head.

To Billy Hardwicke for his help with photographing the cover.

To Dave Fox just for being Dave Fox.

The biggest thanks must go to my old mate Laurence Payne. It was he who pressed me into writing a few years ago and has never doubted my ability, even when I did. His knowledge of all things technical leaves me breathless. I also thank him for his patience in waiting while I got back in the mood during lulls in my enthusiasm.

Contents

Introduction	iv
Acknowledgements	v
The Guttersnipe's Progress	ix
It's All Her Fault	1
'Soldier'	3
Ain't Love Grand!	6
A Shot In The Dark	9
Here Comes The Bride	11
The Birdman Of Chatsworth Road	13
Jack The Lad	19
The Big Freeze	28
The Swinging 60s	32
Up The Market	40
Ducking And Diving!	49
Vote For Ted	56
Never Judge A Book By Its Cover	59
I Don't Believe In Ghosts!	60
The Anointing	64
Nigerian Knees-Up	67
The Biter Bitten	70
A Light In The Dark	72
By George	74
Up Before The Beak Again	80
Brother Billy	82
Fancy Meeting You Here	84
For The Love Of George	86

The Worst Of Times	90
The Funeral	94
Some Time Later	96
Moving On	98
Moving Further On	99
Tales Of The Old Paint Pot	101
The Road To Hollywood	111
My Hero	117
You Lucky People	119
The Long And The Short Of It!	123
Sound Advice	128
Onwards And Almost Upwards	129
God Bless America!	136
It Might Be Alright On The Night!	139
Dickie	144
The Professor	146
I'm Not Well!	149
"Of All The Community Centres ..."	153
Unity Is Strength!	157
A Bit Different	159
A Bit Of East End History	173
Time Marches On!	176
Glossary	179

Hackney Empire
MARE STREET, HACKNEY
Box Office Tel. 01 985 2424
SATURDAY 14th FEBRUARY at 8.p.m.
CHATS PALACE MUSIC HALL PROUDLY PRESENTS A
St. Valentine's
VARIETY
NIGHT
A Benefit for Hackney Empire Preservation Trust
ANN SHELTON
GEORGE WILLIAMS
"I'm Not Well"
KENT BAKER
DEBBIE PEYTON
TONY LOCANTRO & HIS BAND
DICKIE DOWNES
MAUDIE "SPOONS"
SYD MARX
The PLASTIC PEARLIES
Compered By Hackney's Own
DEREK JAMESON
of B.B.C. Radio and T.V.
Tickets £3.50 £2.50 (O.A.P's Unemployed Children)

THE GUTTERSNIPE'S PROGRESS

At an age when some people decide to settle down to being old and past it I discovered the joy of writing. I have always been an avid talker or as some say, a gasbag with plenty of tales to tell, so my mate, Laurence Payne, took me to one side and told me to keep my mouth shut and my hands on the keyboard and write it all down. The result was my first serious attempt at authorship, TALES OF THE OLD EAST END. Read it at 'www.tales-of-the-old-east-end.co.uk'.

I was highly surprised by how easy I found it to compose the stories and how much I enjoyed the process, and I was thrilled by the reactions of the readers of my website so here I am carrying on the searching of the corners of my over-crowded brain to bring you the next slice of my life.

If you have read my previous Tales, you will remember that, as a small boy, I was humiliated and bullied by a sadistic teacher. It was him who continuously insulted me by calling me an East End Guttersnipe and telling me how much he despised me and the likes of me. He put a massive chip on my shoulder.

Most of these tales take place in East London and in particular the Chatsworth Road and surrounding areas of Hackney. Being born and bred in this area I regard it as 'my manor' and after all these years still love it. There is no finer place!

IT'S ALL HER FAULT

I blame my Mum! It's all her fault! Ever since I was a small kid she had told me to "stand up for yourself, don't let anyone take liberties with you and if anyone hits you, hit them back and don't forget to speak up for yourself". She drummed this into me over and over again, it was alright for her, she had a fire in her belly and a fear of no-one.

Many years later, on one cold December day me and three other soldiers marched along a lane heading for the local railway station. This was a special day, all four of us had just been demobbed from the army after serving our two years National Service and now we were outside of the barracks and as free as birds. None of us had met before, but if there was one thing that the army had taught us it was to realise that we were all in this together, so we shouted and laughed loudly and stupidly spoke of what we would do if any bloody Sergeant ever shouted at us again. It was then we spotted him, a particularly hard sergeant who stood on a corner, he swayed back and forward on his heels, all Blanco and bulled up boots, as he stared at us with a menacing sneer on his battered face. My old mum's constant advice rang in my head so what else could I do? It was too much of a temptation. I just had to mimic his regimental manner and tell him what a bastard he was. Of course my ex-brothers in arms spurred on by my verbal frontal attack formed a reinforcement squad and joined in. Our sense of rebellion disappeared as soon as he shouted, as only a British Army sergeant could, "You men. Get yourself over here and stand to attention when I talk to you!" Our short lived bravado slipped away as we did exactly what he told us to and kept our big mouths shut. "So, you think that you are civilians now do you? Well, you stupid lot, your demob date is tomorrow so you are all still soldiers. That means that I can put you on a charge and have you locked up in the guard-room, and if you are not soldiers then I can knock your bloody heads off for taking the piss out of me!" I decided that perhaps my mum was not always right and we all trudged on to the station with the wind taken out of our sails. It was then I realised that the crafty Sergeant was purposely standing outside of the barracks just to goad us and give us a final kick up the kitbag.

As I sat on the London-bound train watching the green fields sliding by I never had one thought about the future but I had a slight sadness about not being a soldier any more. After all I had enjoyed every moment of my military service. I had been to many exotic places and had adventures that I could only have dreamed of, met many interesting people and been very proud. At that time, Britannia ruled the waves and much of the lands of the world. These lands were shown in red on the maps, and I had visited quite a few of them. This travel and experience had, I thought, made a man of me.

All of this sorrow melted away as I thought of spending my days with the love of my life and with my large family in Hackney.

'SOLDIER'

I was only out of the army for a day or two, Christmas was looming, my pocket was empty, so I simply walked across the road to a large factory and got a job labouring in the massive yard.

When I was taken on by the yard manager he warned me that the work was hard and I needed to be strong enough to do it. Huh! Me strong enough? Of course I was, so I looked at him slightly disgusted and said "I have just come out of the army, P.T. every day and marching for miles, no need to worry about me." I had a feeling that he had heard this sort of thing before as he gave me a knowing look when he walked away.

I started work the following morning, no need to hang about, and was introduced to the 'heavy mob,' the yard labourers. I reminded them that I had only a couple of days ago been released from the army, so I was immediately given the nick name 'Soldier'. If I was expecting them to be a gang of tough, muscle-bound hard men then I was to be disappointed, what I met was the puniest, oldest, strangest gaggle of oddballs that you can imagine.

The foreman was called Tiny. This was not some ironic play on words because he was a giant of a man but because he was about 4 feet 8 inches tall. He was also in his late sixties and had a wheezy chest. Among the handful of 'past their sell-by' codgers was Bill, another ancient, scrawny, stooped bloke with a perpetual damp dog-end in his mouth. He constantly sang the old song 'She was a Sweet Little Dickie Bird' replacing the words 'Tweet, tweet, tweet' with 'Chip, chip, chip'. Sulking in the corner was a tall, soppy, nerdy young bloke called Mick, and most bizarre of all was Mitto. The very odd but likeable Mitto was a Venezuelan black man. He was well spoken, educated and well read but he was living in a world of his own. He would often have a conversation with someone that we could not see. He read books most of the time and used a large pencil to cross out single words, paragraphs and often whole pages, he would then scribble his own notes in the margins. He was a large fine-looking man with some strange mystical charisma about him. He told me that he went to the more arty and wealthy West End and read palms, told fortunes and cast spells, he claimed to be paid well for this. I believed him.

However, simple day to day things baffled him. Once he was standing in front of a red hot pot-bellied stove, reading his book as usual, unaware that his trousers were burning, I threw water over his legs and he barely stopped reading. Another time when he was pushing a very squeaky wheelbarrow I stopped him and put a drop of oil on the axle that immediately silenced the squeak. He was amazed and suggested that I had got rid of an evil spirit that was living in the barrow.

This rag-tag army of has-beens did not impress me at all, that was until the hard work began. The store was full of parcels of materials that weighed one hundredweight each and when a lorry load of them arrived they all had to be unloaded by hand, carried to the storage area and stacked. This 'one foot in the grave' gang shuffled up to the lorry, simply lifted the parcels as if they were newspapers and carried them on their shoulders to the store, all the time chatting away and with old Bill puffing on his never-ending dog end. Then it was my turn to lift the load and to show them what a soldier could do. I marched up to the lorry like some kind of military hero and raised my arms to take the 'piffling' parcel hoping that they were going to be suitably impressed.

As soon as the weight was placed on my shoulder the pain began, and as I continued my head spun and I got out of breath. The Heavy Mob continued all day but after an hour I was knackered and defeated. "Take a blow son, you're not used to it" said the kindly old Bill in between 'Chip, Chips'

'SOLDIER'

I had thought that I was better than them seeing as I had just come out of the army, but in my conceit I had completely overlooked the fact that this band of ancient, weedy brothers were all ex-servicemen who had fought in the war. Old George our yard cleaner had served in the first world war, being mentioned in despatches for gallantry in the trenches.

I vowed not to be arrogant again. THAT is when I became a man!

AIN'T LOVE GRAND!

Being back in the arms of my beautiful girl friend was blissful, we couldn't get enough of each other, the more that I saw her the more I loved her. We had been together for a few years and she had faithfully waited for me to serve my Queen and country, but the thought of marriage never entered my head, I was much too young I thought.

Christmas was approaching and she sent me an elaborate card wishing me a Merry Christmas and sending me her undying love, Ah Lovely!

Then inside I saw a handwritten inscription, it was a poem. It read:

> 'We've been together for many years
> and I know that you're a sticker
> But I think it's time that you took the plunge,
> and went to see the vicar.'

Oh gord blimey! She meant it! It was a shock to me but I was thrilled and delighted but what should I do? In the same post was a letter from the War Office, perhaps they wanted me to go back into the Kate Karney and save some far-off colony or the other, surely not! I opened the envelope slowly and the answer to my dithering mind fell onto the table, it was a Post Office money order for the breathtaking sum of 46 pounds 12 shillings and 9 pennies. This was the savings and barrack room breakages money that was stopped every week from our meagre army wages, and to me it was a small fortune. It was a sign that someone somewhere wanted us to get married, so not to waste time I took her to where all good East Enders took their loved ones.

We went to the fabulous Black Lion Yard in Whitechapel! This small yard, not much more than an alley, was rather seedy and in need of a spruce-up but it was full of little Jewish run jewellery shops. Seedy or not it was magical, this is where all respectable Jews bought their jewellery and silver candlesticks. The tiny shops were crammed together each one displaying a window full of sparkling gold, silver and diamond encrusted jewellery.

The yard, known as the East End's Hatton Garden, also had a few book shops and in one corner a canny Welshman called Evans had a dairy with, believe it or not, a small herd of cows. These cows gave good 'kosher' milk and the astute Mr. Evans had a sign outside written in Yiddish, it simply said "Milch, frish fun di ku". I will let you work the translation out.

We walked up and down the yard trying to decide which one to enter when a little old jeweller simply held the door of his shop open for us, we felt obliged to go in, he had made our minds up for us. He greeted us in Yiddish and smiled as he said "Don't tell me, you want an engagement ring."

We were charmed by him. He spoke with a German accent and I guess that he was one of the many refugees from Hitler's hatred. He knew what to do, he simply stood by smiling sincerely as we pondered over the trays of rings until we eventually picked the one that we wanted. The old charmer seemed so pleased for us as he stood in the doorway when we left. "Mazel Tov" he said and as I had gone to school just a few yards away from his shop I was able to reply "Zie mir gezunt." He was pleased.

We were floating on air as we returned home, how romantic to simply get a cheque and immediately get engaged, there was a touch of Gretna Green about it. It was an instant decision that thrilled both of us. On entering my mum and dad's home we gushed "Look. We have got engaged, do you like the ring?" My dad looked so pleased as he embraced us, my young sister got excited and my mum ... well, she glared at us with her face turned inside out. "Why didn't you tell us that you were getting engaged?" she blurted, "Why the secrecy?"

"But we didn't know ourselves, it was a spur of the moment thing" we replied. "Well I don't think it's right" she insisted. "Do you want to see the ring?" we said as the door slammed, but our question remained unanswered.

Well I did say that she was fiery!

A SHOT IN THE DARK

I was given a job inside the factory and taught to operate a large machine, it was quite a skillfull job so I got a pay rise. What with my heavier pay packet and a lot of overtime I was able to squirrel away a nice bit of money and in just over a year we had enough to think of tying the knot. We decided on a date that was a couple of days before the tax year ended, so ensuring a tax rebate. Well, it would have been a shame not to take advantage of the Tax man and then put it down to romance.

The date was set and in no time the wedding day was upon us, but never mind the wedding I had the stag night to organise. Well, when I say organise that was an exaggeration. A lot of my many cousins and mates simply met up in a local pub and we 'pub-crawled' around some of the liveliest pubs in Hackney and to the notorious Regency Club. These pubs were a joy to visit, all had entertainment of some kind, singers, comics and drag artistes, the only disadvantage was that they closed at 11 o' clock. However, this being Hackney there was an answer to this beer starvation - unlicenced drinking clubs. They served drink until the sun came up. The pubs and certainly the Regency Club were very plush and tastefully furnished but these other clubs were just cellars beneath some dilapidated shop and were bloody smelly and dirty, but they dished up the booze whenever you wanted it.

We all rather noisily entered the side door of such a shop and squeezed down a narrow passage and down some even narrower rickety stairs. The smell of stale beer, damp plaster and cheap perfume hung in the air, I didn't like it. It was as dark as night in the tiny room, I guessed that the gaff was so disgustingly dirty that it was cheaper to turn off the lights rather than clean it up. In those days there were lots of villains about, all bragging that they knew

'The Twins' or were related to them and a lot of the dodgy customers eyed us up through the smoky darkness. My dislike of the place grew stronger. How could we make a move for the door without losing face, what excuse could we make to the scar-faced hard man on the door? We all shuffled about, dillying and dallying when fate took an unexpected hand, a shot rang out!!! No thought of face saving now, we were out of that dump like a shot from a gun (sorry about that) and down the road to the safety of our beds. I know that you want details of the pistol shot, but sorry, we never hung about long enough to find out. We didn't want to get involved in such things, after all we had more scary times to face tomorrow, a Wedding!

HERE COMES THE BRIDE

The divine day dawned and I got out of bed as fresh as a week old bottle of milk. I washed and dressed and noted that I was calm and collected, not even a slight twitch of anxiety - that was until there was a hammering on our door. I opened it and there stood my best man, my cousin Fred. He was a bundle of nerves, stuttering and stammering and hopping from one foot to another. He came in and discovered that he had lost his ability to hold a conversation, but not to worry I couldn't stop talking, so perhaps I was nervous after all. Fred produced a bottle of scotch that we swigged at, just for medicinal purposes of course.

    I could not get my beautiful wife-to-be off of my mind, was she suffering from the same problem as me and Fred? I couldn't wait to see her in all her finery so when my cousin Charlie turned up with a car to take me to the church I bundled us all into the motor and told Charlie to put his foot down.

    Inside the church all the mighty Walker tribe and our neighbours had assembled, there was that unmistakeable murmur of twenty or so muted conversations going on. I could hear my dad and my uncles deep in discussion as they studied greyhound racing form and some were complaining that this bloody wedding was depriving them of their Saturday night's dog racing at Clapton Stadium. Me and Fred stood in silence and suddenly all the murmuring stopped. After what seemed like ages the organ struck up the Bridal March and we could hear the rustling of a wedding dress. I was nervous about turning round to see, but I did and there I saw a vision of beauty and grace, it was my blushing bride with her dad Charlie and her four pretty young bridesmaids. I went weak at the knees. We gazed into each others eyes as the vicar started the service. My wife to be, always a particular woman, held my hand and whispered

"Look at the dirt on his dog collar, and I think he has been drinking." Sure enough, his collar was a fine shade of mature yellow and a strong whiff of Scotch wafted in our direction. We squeezed each other's hands in an effort to stop laughing, but the vicar never seemed to notice our stifled giggles as he chuntered through the service safe inside his alcoholic haze.

We posed for photos outside the church and even more friends and neighbours arrived to shout wishes of luck to us, that was the best part of the ceremony for me. Then two ancient but classy Rolls-Royces pulled up and the new Mr. and Mrs. Walker climbed into the first one, the four young bridesmaids and Charlie climbed into the second one. We looked at each other and my heart skipped a beat.

The wedding reception was a typical East London affair, 150 guests, numerous crates of beer, 6 mountains of sandwiches, quite a few tearful relatives, a four piece band, three arguments, two scuffles and one pair of highly delighted love birds.

That week we spent our honeymoon in a place that was close to both our hearts … Hackney!

Soon after we moved into a cosy flat in another splendid place … Chatsworth Road!

THE BIRDMAN OF CHATSWORTH ROAD

When I think back to my childhood I realise that my introduction to birds and animals was a natural part of East London life.Many people kept chickens and rabbits in the back yard to supplement their meat ration and we were no exception. From being a small kid I got great pleasure from the sights, sounds and even the smell of our very own farmyard fowls. My dad went into the army, me and mum did our bit for the war effort by keeping up the meat and egg production, and at the same time sticking up two fingers to Herr Hitler. I soon learned to spot when a chicken was poorly or injured and what to do to get it back to scratch, and became pretty good at rearing the day chicks that we bought from a stall in Chatsworth Road market.

Peace was declared and dad returned to his bit of rustic heaven in Hackney and to the comfort of his flock of egg-laying friends. I was no longer a toddler so it was time to be taught the knowledge that dad had acquired in a lifetime of keeping birds, and I was a keen student. Then dad relived his childhood by taking up the addictive hobby of Pigeon keeping, and I followed willingly. By the time that I was ten I was a seasoned fancier with all the knowledge of breeding, feeding and flying these fascinating birds.

In my teens, the Sunday Bird and Animal market in Club Row and Sclater Street was in its prime. It is now seen as being cruel and exploitative, but for me and thousands of others who flocked in from all over London it was a magnet. All kinds of birds, reptiles and animals were displayed and were possible to buy within our meagre incomes, so it was no surprise when the more exotic birds caught my imagination and prompted me to get dad to make me an aviary.

National Service ended my hobby, but as soon as I returned and got married the itch needed scratching again. As newlyweds we moved into a small flat above a shop at 91 Chatsworth Road, a cosy little place with a back garden, so within a short time I had made a shed and a small aviary and within a year my tiny finches were producing plenty of chicks. Our back garden was accessible from the street and mums would bring their babies in to see the dicky birds and workers in the furniture factory that shared our entrance would bring in visitors and sit in our garden to drink their tea, it was a very happy time.

One day I had a knock on my door, it was a mum with her little boy who held up a small box with a poor old sparrow that was placed on the newspaper that lined the box, the unfortunate bird just lay there with his eyes shut and was breathing laboriously. It was obvious that it would not last very long but mum's concerned look on her face and her teary-eyed son made me say with great authority that "he will be alright, leave him with me and I will look after him". Dear old Jack Sparrow silently slipped away and I buried him in my garden, a few days later I had a note pushed into my letterbox saying Thank You for saving the little bird. I felt like a fraud, but just a little proud at the same time. I don't know if this mum spread the word about my miraculous curing abilities but more concerned people called in from time to time with sick or needy birds and a few times I somehow managed to get them better. I quickly learnt that keeping a sick bird still and warm was the best way to treat them. I learnt how to trim cage birds' nails and beaks and realised that I got a big thrill from seeing the grateful looks on the owners' faces.

At that time most people had a budgerigar or a canary in a cage in their front rooms and cared passionately for them, and from time to time I was asked to look after Dicky or Joey while they went away on holiday. Dicky or Joey also enjoyed the couple of weeks holiday spent in my shed within sight and sound of all my birds. Once a year I had the pleasure of caring for a lovely talking mynah bird, a bird that filled our bit of Chatsworth Road with exotic and tropical sounds and a few choice words, causing the workers from the factory to stand in my garden for hours making strange bird sounds back to the puzzled songster.

On the other side of the road, in the first flat in Chatsworth Estate, lived two nice old ladies who adored their two Budgies. One day they waved to me across the road to come over and take a look at their beloved birds, and not without good cause, both of them had extremely overgrown nails and beaks. The nails were so long that landing on the perch was so difficult that they spent most of the time on the floor of the cage, and the beaks had grown to almost a circle making eating almost impossible. Both birds were, as a result, in poor condition. I trimmed the nails and nervously cut most of the misshapen beaks away.

They had got this way because they had nothing to wear away the offending beaks and nails, so I put a cuttlefish bone in the cage and cut some twigs from an apple tree and hung them inside as well. Within a few days both the precious little darlings were chirping away and looking more like Budgies should do. One of the old girls crossed the road to knock on my door to give me a bag of sweets for my kids and a Thank You note addressed to 'The Bird Man'. That was it, it was now my title!

My finches continued to produce young birds, and the rabbits that I had foisted upon me seemed to be in competition with them, but not to worry, I just walked them across the road to Johnny Lambert's Pet Shop at 90 Chatsworth Road where Johnny sold them for me, and being prone to exaggeration told his customers of my ability to cure every known illness that birds could contract. In fact I was getting confident of my abilities. Once when one of my tiny hen finches sat on the floor of the aviary with all of her feathers fluffed up and a look of resignation about her, I somehow thought that she might be egg bound. That meant that she had an egg inside her that would not pass through the narrow vent, so remembering my dad's advice I put her in a warm place, smeared her vent with oil and held her in the steam from a kettle. Within a short time the egg popped out and in an even shorter time my brave little hen composed herself, began twittering and got stuck into the bird seed just as if nothing had happened. I had never had such a feeling of happiness and satisfaction before or since, my wife and kids stood there with great big smiles on their faces. It was pure joy.

   Little did I know that an even more demanding but satisfying event was to take place. Again it started with knock on my door, when I opened it there stood an anxious mum and her kids with a rusty old budgie cage, inside the cage was what looked like a messy bundle of grass and twigs. Mum spoke up with tension in her voice, "The caretaker at Rushmore School told me to come to you, look, we found these in the road, they must have fallen from a tree, what can we do with them?" I took the cage into my shed and removed the tea towel that had been carefully placed over it for protection. Inside the cage was a bird's nest and inside the nest were three very small chicks, "I have been told that they are greenfinches" Mum said, "will they be alright?" I gazed at the helpless chicks with a mixture of wonder and uncertainty. The nestlings were only a day or two old, completely featherless and weak, they struggled unsuccessfully to hold up their large heads and their huge black eyes were yet to open. Two of them wriggled and opened their beaks in expectation of being fed, but the third one just lay in the nest hardly moving. I was just about to say "Leave them to me, they will be alright" when reality made me keep my thoughts to myself, I didn't know what to do but could not let the concerned mum and kids know, so following my natural instincts I went into the garden and looked for insects and small worms. They were easy to find, and when I gently offered them to the gaping mouths they disappeared with a gulp. That was it, I instantly felt responsible for these unfortunate little things, I uttered the words "Leave them to me." Mum and the kids went away and only then did I realise the amount of time that I would spend nursing my adopted youngsters.

Later that day the poor little runt of the clutch stopped breathing and I buried it alongside all the other birds that could not be saved, but the other two just kept opening their beaks as wide as they could. No amount of spiders and greenfly seemed to satisfy them so I walked across to Johnny Lambert's Pet Shop to buy some Canary Rearing Food. This powder-like substance was mixed with water to make a paste that the greedy pair scoffed with relish. I always finished each meal with a dessert of insects and a few drips of water.

I don't know how the squeaking orphans felt but I was so pleased with the whole experience.

At this time I was working long hours in a factory in the now trendy Fish Island, Old Ford, so giving the infants a meal at frequent and regular times seemed a problem. The company went by the splendid name of The Britannia Folding Box Company and I operated a big machine which was situated in the corner of a huge room full of machines and lots of workers but I managed every day to sneak the cage into the factory and hide it in a cupboard. As the mighty machine clattered away I fed the hungry duo who by now were sprouting feathers and sitting up squeaking even more loudly. Of course the many women who worked there would gather round the cupboard ooohing and aaahing and speaking to them as if they were human babies, making me worried about being found out. The manager of the factory was a straight-laced, no nonsense bloke who only cared about his daily production output so I steered clear of him, but unfortunately one day he silently walked up behind me as I was feeding the trouble makers. His stern face never showed any indication of what he was thinking, we both stood there in silence. "Well, finish off their dinner" he said "and get on with your work."

The following day I had a visit from the Managing Director. "Can I see the birds?" he said. He was enthralled by the chirpy pair and gave me a pat on the back as he left. From then on there was a steady stream of office workers popping in to see the stars of The Britannia Folding Box Co. When a Director of a Danish company visited the factory he was given a tour of the factory and an audience with our heroes.

By now they were fully fledged, and had become handsome greenfinches. They were ready to fly the nest, so with some anxiety I placed the cage on the wall of my backyard and opened the door. As they looked around I had no sadness because I just knew that they would return to me just like all the hand-reared creatures I had read about in books, but with no warning the two of them bolted out of the cage like shot from a gun and flew straight out of sight without even a backward glance, never to be seen again.

That's gratitude for you!

JACK THE LAD

We spent the first ten years of our married life in the cosy little flat above a shop in Chatsworth Road and very happy days they were too, mostly because of the good neighbours that we had. Beneath our flat was a washing machine repair shop run by the very friendly and helpful George, behind us was Strong's Furniture Factory whose owner Bill Strong and his twenty or so workers all became our friends, but without any doubt the icing on the congenial cake was the family who lived next door, Jack and Lal and their two kids. We got on like a house on fire and shared many good, bad and mostly hilarious times. It is Jack that I would like to concentrate on today.

 Jack was a tall, slim, bald-headed bloke, his high cheek-boned expressionless face hid the fact that he had a kind, helpful nature, a wicked sense of humour, and a blatant disregard of rules and regulations. He wasn't too keen on authority of any kind and was an expert in acting in ignorance when it suited him, all together a joyful and exciting bloke to be around. I never knew what would be the outcome of our many dealings.

 Jack was a refuse collector back in the days when they were pleased to be called Dustmen. He had an eye for objects that might be turned into hard cash and was never too bothered if they had been discarded or not, but always insisted that they had been 'thrown out with the dust'. He would amass a nice collection of desirable objects d'art and swear that they had been given to him because they were no good, but these useless relics would suddenly become priceless antiques when a potential buyer arrived. It was an education to watch him just stand by his stash with that poker-faced look of ignorance working its almost wordless magic on the 'expert' buyer. Most questions were answered with a puzzled response of "I don't know mate" giving the impression that the buyer was dealing with an idiot. Idiot he was not.

Among the many dodges that he got me involved in was the removal of unwanted items or, to put it another way, clumsy oversized furniture. I have always had a van, so when some of his clients asked him to take away these cumbersome objects he would say "Sorry but they are too big for the dustcart, but I know someone who will take it away for a small consideration". That someone was, of course, me, so we would call in the evening to quote a not so small consideration and remove the surplus furniture. I always asked Jack "Where are we going to dump this crap?" He always replied "I have got just the place, don't worry about it". But I should have known that the straight-faced answer was just pie in the sky. A few times he guided me to an unknown place in East London and told me to park by the pavement while he went round the corner to speak to the recipient of the junk. I thought more than once that he was asking for a money for the rubbish, but I was wrong. If only it had been as innocent as that. When he returned we unloaded the unsightly toot on to the pavement ready to take it round to the 'customer'. It was at this point that Jack grabbed me by the collar and pushed me into the cab of the van and shouted "Come on, let's piss off as quick as we can" and the tyres screeched as we sped off down the road leaving an unwanted monument blocking the footpath. Once it was even worse than this, we had pulled up outside a row of three-storied houses and the offending monstrosities had been unloaded onto the pavement when Jack saw that the door to a basement flat was open. He called into the door and a woman came out. "Hello Ma" he said. "Your old man has bought you a new three piece suite, where would you like it?"

The woman was thrilled to have new furniture. "Put it in the front room" she said, with a look of surprised pleasure on her face. The dark brown, ugly armchairs were carried down the basement stairs and with a bit of a struggle we got them into the required room, then it was the turn of the even uglier four seater settee. It was as heavy as lead, and when we tried to get it through the front door it was evident that it would not go without a fight.

"Give it a bloody great shove" said Jack and that is what we did but now it was well and truly stuck, we couldn't move it either way. There we were stuck outside the flat unable to get in, and there was the rather dismayed lady of the house stuck inside unable to get out.

It was then that Jack again grabbed me by the collar and thrust me into the van with the immortal words "Quick, let's piss off". And that's what we did!

Jack, like many others, would be open to offers of 'something cheap' and one of these offers saw him and his brother in law, along with their kids, picking up something from North London. The 'gear' was loaded into the boot of the car, the two men sat in the front seat and the kids in the rear seats, and they all made their way back to Chatsworth Road.

On the way back they somehow got entangled in a local carnival among all the highly decorated floats, walking groups, Caribbean dancers and marching bands. This unexpected meeting meant that they could not do anything but drive at the same speed as the parade, but it gave them the chance to begrudgingly join in the fun. Suddenly there was a drumming on the boot of the car, a woman was shouting in a frantic way so Jack got out to find to his horror that his four year old son had somehow managed to open the rear door of the car and fall out onto the road. Jack was concerned about his kid and just as concerned about the contents of the boot, but a quick examination of the boy showed that, apart from a tiny graze and a stain on his shirt he was fine, if a bit shaken up. As he was being hurriedly bundled into the car a Police Sergeant appeared, looking worried about the possible consequences of the mishap. The sergeant insisted on calling an ambulance to take them all to the hospital but Jack did not fancy this at all, he was torn between his concern for his boy and the fear that the copper would poke his nose into the boot. In some way he managed to reassure the copper that the boy would be fine and that he had to get home because his mum would worry about him being late, all the time being aware of the very 'warm' contents of the boot. The sergeant was convinced and called a colleague to escort the car from the carnival parade and speed it past all the other vehicles bogged down in the festivities.

Another time Jack took my 5 year old boy Glenn and his son Mark out in the car somewhere, they returned along with two of Mark's cousins smiling all over their faces. I knew that they had been having a good time because they were all singing a song at the tops of their voices. It seems that Jack had taught them all a song about a certain man called 'Bollocky Bill from Stamford Hill'. Typical Jack!

If you are a fan of sweet little pussy cats that have silk bows around their necks and sleep on beds of rose petals then I suggest that you skip this next tale.

Bill Strong, who owned the furniture factory was a man whose looks belied his soft nature, he was in his late 60s with dyed hair, a pencilled moustache, a camel-hair coat and a rusty Mercedes car. He had all the swagger and manner of a hard-bitten businessman and an abrupt way of speaking when dealing with other traders and his workers, but I knew him as extremely over-sentimental, emotional and soft-hearted. Often as he passed my garden and my menagerie, he would come in and stand in silence with a lump in his throat, then he would put his arm around my shoulder and heap blessings upon me saying that I was like a breath of fresh air to him and that I would get my reward in Heaven for my kindness to my little creatures. Sometimes he would attempt to leave, but something would bring him back to bless me again and put a pound note in my hand to 'treat your kids'.

One day me and Jack were standing in the garden when a very troubled Bill appeared carrying a chocolate box that he handled with reverence, again his arm went around my shoulder and he appealed to me to help him. His croaky voice and his moist eyes made it impossible to say no to his request, whatever it was. He went on to tell me that his precious cat had just delivered 7 kittens but, to his great heartbreak, one of them was born dead and here it was in the chocolate box swathed carefully in that soft paper that you used to find in expensive chocolates. Again he went into the 'breath of fresh air' routine, told me what to expect to get when I got to Heaven and, struggling with the lump in his throat, begged me to find a nice peaceful spot in my 'lovely' garden to lay the pathetic pussy to rest. Of course I promised to do this, and I meant it. Bill choked back a tear and silently left, me and Jack stood in silence, then Jack gently took the Chocolate box from my hand and gazed at it, giving out a sympathetic cry of "Aaaah". Three times the sorrowful 'Aaaah' was repeated, followed by what seemed to be a silent prayer. Then, out of the blue, the feline coffin was tossed into the air and received an almighty kick that sent it flying over about three gardens never to be seen again. Jack's straight face never altered as he said "Silly bastard!" I didn't know whether to laugh or cry. I laughed uncontrollably.

Always willing to get our hands on a bob or two, me and Jack took on any jobs that were offered to us. These jobs that we did after work covered a wide range, gardening, clearance, removals and painting and decorating. We had a run on decorating when lots of West Indians bought up the then unwanted big houses in Hackney. When we finished one house we would be recommended to another owner, and we soon got nearly proficient in the art of pasting and papering. I had half an idea about it but Jack never had a clue, he never knew one end of a brush from another but he was a willing worker and a good labourer and, blimey, did we have some laughs!

A few times we were asked to look at a garden just to tidy up but we would offer to redesign the garden just as though we knew what we were doing. I would walk around making suggestions that I had just plucked from thin air, and Jack would nod his head wisely in agreement, then he would bend down, pick up a handful of soil and run it through his fingers, and proclaim "Good soil here". The customers were so impressed. They thought that he was a local Alan Titchmarsh.

One decorating job that we did was for Bill Strong. Bill lived with his wife of many years in some leafy part of Woodford, his almost middle aged son worked in the factory along with Bill's brother, and Bill also had a retail shop near Mare Street Hackney. The shop, where he sold his three piece suites direct to the public, had quite a nice roomy flat above it and Bill asked us to brighten it up for the tenant. This tenant, a voluptuous blonde woman in her late twenties was the object of Bill's rather ancient desire and somehow he had managed to father a small child with her much to the disapproval of his son and brother, not to mention his hard-done-by wife. Bill still lived in Woodford with his wife and spent the opening hours of the shop with his fancy bit. His wife, upset by the arrangements, became depressed and bent Bill's ear quite a lot, but it seems that Bill's love for her kept him living with and caring about her. Things came to a head one day when a confrontation with his wife led to him 'reassuring' her in bed before he went to work and then 'reassuring' the young mum at least once, then going home at lunchtime and once again 'reassuring' his wife before returning to the factory. He pulled the trusty Merc up outside the gates and staggered across the pavement but unfortunately never reached the entrance, he simply collapsed in an exhausted heap in the middle of the pavement. There was not much sympathy from his disgruntled family members and workers and all Jack could say was "Cor, what a way to go!" You will be pleased to hear that Bill didn't go!

In those days if you had a large lorry it was compulsory to leave a light on it during the hours of darkness. Bill Strong had a large furniture van, a pantechnicon, (that's a name that you don't hear much these days) and entrusted me to put a clip-on lamp on it every night. He gave me a key to the van so that I could store the lamp away, but a key in my hand and an empty van was too much of a temptation for us when a big job was offered. One Sunday morning I started up the huge lorry and drove it out into Chatsworth Road when the familiar sight of Bill Strong's rusty Merc came into view. Bill slammed on his brakes, flashed his headlights, jumped out and said "What the **** do you think you are doing with my motor?" "It's alright Bill" I stammered, while I was searching my brain for an answer. "I noticed that the battery was flat this morning so I bump started it down the hill to charge up the battery, I didn't want you to come in to a dead battery tomorrow". Bill's anger slipped away at once and that moist-eyed look returned, "What a good boy you are, you are like a breath of fresh air, etc. etc." His arm went round my shoulder again as he slipped another pound note into my hand, Jack stood on the pavement with that familiar blank look on his face just as though it was nothing to do with him.

I have many fond memories of the very kind Bill and the boys of the factory that I hold dearly.

Jack could make an ordinary event into something special just with a bit of school boy naughtiness. One idle afternoon I was pottering about in the garden when one of my kids asked me why we never had any baby bunnies like we used to have. The answer was obvious, we only had two rabbits and they were both does, you know, female rabbits, so I told the small gang of kids who always seemed to be around me, about the birds and the bees and how I needed a daddy rabbit, a buck, to weave the magic spell. One of the kids who lived across the road in Lockhurst Street, piped up "My friend who lives next to me has got a rabbit, it's a big one too". It sounded like it could be a buck so, urged on by Jack and the kids, I decided that there was no time like the present. I picked up a sack and set off to investigate the likelihood of a liaison between the bunnies. Jack was now enjoying himself by getting the kids excited and as our little mob passed my sister-in-laws house my nephew and his mates had joined in, the kids getting louder as we approached Daddy Bunny's abode.

I knocked on the door and a lady opened it, luckily she knew me so it was quite easy to explain our shortage in the mating department. I'm not so sure that she was comfortable about me taking away the family pet, but the sight of the excited Jack and his cohorts must have made her unable to say No! I put the big old buck into the sack. "You must always take the buck to the doe" I said, like some kind of a husbandry expert, and off the happy band went back to our backyard. On the way back we picked up a few more members of this gang of potential voyeurs, Jack was beside himself with sheer joy as we passed through the alley and into the garden.

I could see that Jack was bursting to say something vulgar about the situation. He was acting like a naughty schoolboy, so I took the rabbit from the sack and, assuming a school master-like pose, told the kids what was about to happen and why. When I eventually put Mr. Bunny into Miss Bunny's hutch the bemused kids fell silent not knowing what to expect. Our super-stud just sat there without moving, his prospective partner looked at him unimpressed, the silence continued. Suddenly Mr. Buck sprang into life, made a mad leap at her and performed his task in seconds. Jack could not hold himself back. Punching the air he shouted "Go on me old son, give her one!" I don't think the kids understood the expression, well that's what I told myself, but they all gave a loud cheer.

Our little back yard was full of fecundity, we just thought it was natural and normal and my kids grew up with no hang-ups about breeding and childbirth. When my second son, Billy, was about four, we all went to the seaside and we were exploring the rock pools when a little girl called to her Dad "Look, this crab is on top of another one, what are they doing?" Dad looked embarrassed as he cleared his throat and replied "Er, er, they are playing piggybacks". My little Billy never turned a hair as he said "No they are not, they are mating. They will have babies soon" I felt proud of my son and a just a little pleased with myself. If only Jack had been there he may have told him that he was giving her one!"

The natural and normal reproduction was not confined to our backyard because when we, as newly-weds, moved into 91 Chatsworth Road, there were just the two of us but after 10 years of wedded bliss, love and passion we had produced three lovely sons. My boys and my beautiful young wife were the loves of my life, the reason for my happiness and for this being the best time of my life.

My and Jack's families shared many happy days together, I have hundreds of stories that include this straight-faced special individual with his own wicked, wry sense of humour and some of them are suitable to be told in mixed company.

THE BIG FREEZE

This is not a story but is an account of how we coped with an historic bout of severe weather that affected the whole of the British Isles. But never mind the whole of the British Isles, it's our little bit of Chatsworth Road that I was concerned with at the time.

The grim episode began at the beginning of January 1963 with a fall of snow, nothing out of the ordinary, but it made us look forward to the spectacle that it would bring. What we did not expect was the dramatic drop in temperature that accompanied the winterland scenes, it caused the road outside to resemble a skating rink bringing chaos to both pedestrians and motorists and prompting concern about our little baby who was not even a year old.

However the following day a small army of workmen armed with heavy shovels worked their way methodically, and quite swiftly, down Chatsworth Road breaking up the two inch thick sheet of ice that covered the tarmac. The shattered ice was carelessly shovelled into the side of the road up against the many cars that were parked there causing an ice pile about two feet or so in height, but not to worry, these piles would soon melt away. Well that was the plan, but old Mother Nature had plans of her own and the Antarctic temperatures remained until early March and the ice piles became a solid, long-remaining feature. We were not to know this, and the most of London that was in the same position waited patiently for the melt with thousands of vehicles frozen in to the kerbs and small versions of the Alps reducing the width of all the roads.

After a day or two my patience ran out and I got a pickaxe and released my van but this action was not the answer to the problem because the roads and pavements were still as slippery as a greasy eel. This slipperiness made driving very hazardous, even a short journey to the petrol station became an adventure, but being a sensible bloke with many years driving experience I was full of confidence and belief in my ability. In fact I had only been driving for about three years so had never encountered such drastic conditions before. I drove so slowly, just like so many other drivers, that a local trip took hours, it was not worth driving if unnecessary. I accelerated gently, braked even more gently, stayed away from other drivers and generally drove like an old maid, so I almost had control of my van. However I was not prepared for a most unusual incident.

After diligently crawling along with my heart in my mouth, I pulled up at a red light, kept my foot on the brake pedal and the hand brake fully on, but I was aware that the van was still moving. I was stopped on a road with a deep camber to it. Although the brakes held the wheels locked stopping the van from moving forward, they could do nothing to stop it from sliding sideways until it bumped against the kerb. What a feeling of helplessness! I then determined to leave the van at home and walk as much as possible.

I decided that a bit of ice was not going to get the better of me so I got some rags and tied them with twine around my shoes. I figured that the rag would not slip like the rubber soles did. I stepped out on to the icy pavement and, much to my joy, my feet gripped the shiny surface.

Some young boys looked at my odd footwear and laughed out loud, calling me all sorts of weirdo, but I, with a superior tone, told them that *they* were the idiots for not making themselves as safe as me. With a cocky swagger I set off up Chatsworth Road.

My new invention had one weak spot, The twine was a cheap and cheerful product of some back-street Far-Eastern workshop and within a few yards disintegrated, causing the rags to be left behind and me to fall heavily on to my bum. The young boys gave out a loud mickey-taking laugh and I jumped up, threatening to kick them up the High Street. They somehow managed to run away at speed without the use of my second-rate invention.

So began the longest and coldest freeze-up in history.

You may have noticed that many times I have referred to 'our cosy little flat', well it remained cosy, but bloody freezing. Being the last house in the terrace, one of our walls was unprotected making it even more bloody freezing. The bedroom was the coldest room, most morning we woke to find ice curtains and baby's bottle frozen solid.

Our puny electric fire never made the slightest difference to our comfort so I re-installed the fire grate and bought some coal. The glowing fire was an improvement, but only if you sat about nine inches away from it. Then it had the effect of burning your shins until they resembled corned beef but leaving the rest of you to the mercy of Jack Frost's big brother. Soon it was impossible to find any shop that had coal in stock so we burned anything that we could find. There were still a few bomb sites about and I scoured them for any combustible matter. I got my hands on a paraffin heater but paraffin soon became scarce, things were not improving. I was desperate!

Bill Strong's factory still produced three-piece suites, making the wooden frames on site and, more importantly, producing waste wooden offcuts. When I mentioned our plight to some of the boys they were upset that I had never asked them before. As these offcuts were snapped up as soon as they were available, our concerned mates made sure that we got our share every day, so bringing us a good deal of comfort.

The freeze lasted for a couple of months and disappeared as quickly as it came, no more icy nights, wet, cold feet, and no more wet bums (no, not what you are thinking, I lost count of the times that I lost my footing and sat heavily on to the icy pavements).

Just a little foot-note, the small army of shovellers who cleared the ice from the roads were all what we now call Jobseekers. In those days you were not given your dole money if you didn't 'volunteer' for such duties. Please don't mention this to David Cameron.

THE SWINGING 60s

Sex 'n Drugs 'n Rock 'n Roll, Beatlemania, pop stars, groupies and one or two superstars somehow filtered into our little alley in Chatsworth Road. We lived on the first floor and on the second floor was an equally small flat, the pleasant young couple who lived there moved out after a few of years and that's where this sometimes unbelievable tale starts.

The incoming tenant was called David and he was a musician. He had an engaging personality, and it seemed that we would have an interesting time with our new neighbour. He was a very distant relative of Jack's and we soon became friendly with him, his stories of pop stars had us enthralled. We should have been warned when a player-piano turned up and was squeezed up our narrow staircase, damaging the decorating that I had done, but David charmingly apologised profusely and promised to repair the damage. That was the very first of the many empty promises that we had and, with the player-piano thumping out until the early hours, we began to question the enthusiastic welcome we had given him.

Let me at this stage of the proceedings tell you that the outwardly charming David was what my old man would call 'a Holy Friar', a bloody liar to you, so the seemingly incredible facts that follow are a mixture of truth and fantasy. I think that you will guess what is what.

Along came The Beatles and Merseybeat. Music programmes dominated the TV and David was swept up in this exciting time. It is a fact that he joined a band called Jimmy Powell and the 5 Dimensions and that Jimmy and his band had quite a bit of success with a few records and appearances on TV. We saw David a couple of times on Top of the Pops and such programmes, sometimes with The Beatles, The Rolling Stones and other legendary bands. It is also a fact that an unknown Rod Stewart got his first job with Jimmy Powell.

All this truth was of course exaggerated and embroidered upon and provided David with fertile facts that he grew into unbelievable fantasies. For instance, when I complained about the noise that he made late at night he apologised and said that it wasn't him that made the noise but Paul McCartney or Mick Jagger or Joe Cocker or even Roger Moore, and that they were drunk so couldn't help it. He promised to make them come in to apologise to me when they came in next time. He once said that Roger Moore was calling in on him at the weekend but couldn't get a babysitter so would we mind if Moore Junior shared my eldest son's cot while they went round to the pub. I think that you may now have the extent of his daydreaming, so I won't give you any more details of his porky pies.

He drove the minibus for the band and this bus was parked outside in Chatsworth Road with the title 'Jimmy Powell and the 5 Dimensions' emblazoned along its length, causing quite a few young star-struck girls to hang around it waiting to see someone famous. In those days I had long hair and a beard, like many people, and a few times found that these soppy teenagers thought that I was one of the band.

Not content with being a champion fantasist, he was also a tea leaf and con man. He conveniently forgot his wallet when he went shopping in Chatsworth Road and promised most of the shops that he would come straight back with the money, a promise that was as empty as his pockets. When he walked through the market he would have to cross and recross the road to avoid the trusting traders who had been victims of his gift of the gab and 'sincere' charm.

As we both shared a front door, many debtors, bailiffs, and policemen would bang angrily on the solid door. Of course he never responded to the racket so I would go down to talk to them. At least half a dozen times when I turned the latch the door flew inwards and a couple of heavies pinned me to the wall demanding payment. Once two coppers called, he had to produce his driving documents to the local nick but, of course had not bothered. The brawny constables were angry and threatened to jump all over him when they met him. Of course I encouraged them to do more than that and they left cursing him. They called back a few more times, each time getting more and more determined to make mincemeat of him, when finally by some clever ruse of tapping gently on the door he opened up and they all came face to face. I stood in my hallway grinning with satisfaction and waiting for the explosion of anger from the Old Bill, but instead David's slimy charm greeted them. "Hello Boys" he said, "Come in, do you want a cup of tea?" They all went upstairs to the flat above and I waited for the fun to start, but after 10 minutes they all appeared at the door smiling widely. "Nice to see you, boys" said David. "Thanks for the records, Dave" they said. "That's alright, call in any time you are passing" said the crafty bastard. His notorious charm had worked again.

 His bragging bullshit was not confined to Chatsworth Road, now and then he went 'on tour' with the band and who knows what he told to gullible fans that he met in many parts of the country. One encounter with a woman 'up north' led to a disturbed sleep for both me and Jack.

 One dark and rainy night I was deep in blissful slumber when at some unearthly time our door bell rang like a shrill alarm, I jumped out of bed ready to go down to the alley to see just what the emergency was. My wife, always more sensible than me, said "Don't go down to that dark alley without knowing who is down there, be careful!" Realising the wisdom of this statement I stuck my head out of the window and shouted out "Who's ringing that bell, what do you want?" After a minute a scruffy woman carrying a sleeping bag stepped out of the alley and into partial view. "What do you want?" I growled. "I'm looking for David" she said, in a North Country accent. Well you may have guessed that I was not in the best of moods when I answered "Well why are you ringing my bell? Go away and let me sleep". "But he told me to call in on him when I was in London, he is such a nice bloke". "That's your opinion, now go away" I said, getting grumpier by the minute. "But I've got nowhere to go, let me come in and stay with you". "No chance of that" I moaned, but she was not about to give up. "Come down and let me come in to sleep on your floor". "Go away"said I, she was getting desperate now. "I don't want to sleep with you" the cheeky cow said. "I don't remember asking you" was my sharp reply.

She whined on about being tired and uncomfortable but my heart never melted as I said "Who is with you?". "I'm on me own, let me in". I felt sure that there may be someone else lurking in the dark alley so I slammed the window shut as she rang the bell over and over again. Then all went quiet, it seems that she had spotted Jack's doorbell on the other side of our entrance. Up went Jack's bedroom window and our monosyllabic straight-faced mate simply said "Yeah?" "Do you know David?" she said "Yeah" repeated Jack. "He told me to ..." and she repeated her dreary tale of homelessness. "Oh Yeah" was Jack's short reply, and this was his answer to every thing that she boringly chuntered on with. All her pathetic pleas simply sailed over Jack's head and there was not a hint of concern on his straight face.

Eventually she got just weary of pleading. "Can you do me a favour?" she asked, "Yeah" said Jack "When you see David can you tell him that his neighbours are horrible shits?" "Yeah, I will do that" said our Jack as he slammed the window. Me and my wife were laying in bed aching with laughter at Jack's unsympathetic replies to her pleading. I looked out of the window through the curtains to see her cross the pavement with the two blokes who had been hiding in the alley throughout her fruitless imploring. Phew! That was a close one.

Another time our roving troubadour went away on an 'important gig' and seeing that me and liberty-taking David were at loggerheads he gave the keys of his flat to Jack. He asked Jack to pop in and make sure that all was well in his somewhat quirky abode. As soon as David went Jack called me to go up with him to have a nose around, I didn't need asking twice. What we saw filled us with wonder and puzzlement. The flat was extremely small, even smaller than our one and the style of decor was what might be called 'Art Crappo'. The stairs and landing were entirely carpeted, but with off-cuts from the carpet dump, creating a mind numbing mixture of colours and patterns. All the walls and ceilings of the entire flat were papered with centre-fold spreads of naked nubile young women, some of the photos going into details that I can't reveal in this wholesome publication. He had cut the banisters from the steep and narrow staircase making the ascent an adventure in its own right. A fine layer of dust covered most of the furniture and, as befitting such a luxurious dwelling, each room had its own spider sanctuary. As we entered the kitchen we were aware of a 'pen and ink' that turned our stomachs, on closer scrutiny we found unwashed washing up that had more penicillin mould than the Hackney Hospital and as we opened the cupboard under the sink strange alien creatures advanced towards us. These creatures were in fact the shoots from long forgotten potatoes that were desperately searching out the nearest light. In their efforts to find freedom they had acquired a creepy Triffid-like appearance. Something about them made both me and Jack speechless, so we continued our expedition in stunned silence, approaching every cupboard and closet with nervous expectation.

David had always fancied himself as a bit of a cowboy and had a small collection of western paraphernalia that was carelessly displayed about his somewhat eerie abode.

Stetsons and sombreros hung on the wall, a saddle was slung over a chair, bows and arrows stood in the corner and a couple of stuffed birds and a scabby looking fox's head adorned the walls. This fox had a pathetic look upon its face mainly due to the fact that it only had one eye. In pride of place over the fireplace was a handsome

Gunslinger's belt complete with decorative holsters and two revolvers that Wyatt Earp would have been proud of. These revolvers in fact fired ball-bearings, and an open box of these small but deadly missiles sat on the mantelpiece just under the guns.

All this was too much of a temptation for Jack. He took a pistol from its holster, carefully loaded it and stood up with that familiar naughty-boy look upon his face. I feared the worst. It seemed like Wyatt Earp had actually returned and taken over Jack as he caressed the barrel of the pistol looking for a target, then his searching eyes lit upon the mangy fox's head that wonkily hung on the wall just asking to be shot to pieces. The first shot hit the mark causing the fox to jerk into an even more wonky position, the next half a dozen shots moved it about even more until the tatty article fell to the dusty floor. Jack looked possessed as his eyes scanned the room for more victims of his trigger-happy finger, and there they were all lined up on the shelf. David's knick-knacks and ornaments fell foul of the ball bearings one at a time and even some of the naked women on the make-do wallpaper got wounded in the obvious places. By now Jack was in a full flush of gunfire. A chandelier with six bulbs went down in a hail of gunfire and now every bulb in the flat joined them in their journey to Boot Hill, followed by the very scary looking stuffed birds. The still silent Jack very unusually had the hint of a smug smirk on his normally blank face, and even I stood in silence, not believing what I had just seen.

"Blimey Jack, what will he say when he comes home and sees all this damage?" I nervously asked. I should have known what his answer was going to be. He just stood there and calmly said "Fuck him" as he carried on demolishing everything breakable in the gaff. David returned and never mentioned the devastation of his strange museum, but he did continue with his noisy record playing and the thumping of his ancient player piano. If only Jack had shot him instead of an innocent wonky fox!

Things were coming to an inevitable head, our peace of mind had been ruined and our health was threatened. In return I threatened him with violence and the local council but he knew that I was not

a violent man and he had no fear of any local authority, confident that his smarmy charm would protect him. One Sunday morning we had a visit from Pam's sister Maureen and her husband. Her sister was not the timid, gentle woman that Pam was and her husband was a massive bloke with a 'history' and a reputation. Maureen was appalled by the noise and angered by the effect it was having on her younger sister, so picked up a broom and laid into the ceiling.

Almost immediately David came to the door and for the first time was on the offensive, but he was no match for Maureen. Although she was just about 7 stone she was a bit of a nutcase who would stand no nonsense. She advanced with the broom and a long list of threats and calling David every name that is unprintable here. His responses never stood a chance against Maureen's mad tirade.

Just then a woman who had moved in with David after his wife had left him poked her nose around the door frame hurling abuse. Maureen's response has gone down in family history. "You can shut your mouth, fucking second hand Rose. One more sound from you and you will get to the bottom of the stairs quicker than you came up". The door slammed in defeat, David and Second Hand Rose went to the front of the flat and gazed on to Chatsworth Road. On the pavement stood 20 stone of Maureen's husband staring back at them with a look that would strip paint. He shook his fist at David and Second hand Rose. They stepped back from the window and quickly closed the curtains.

The following day David moved out, we have never seen him since!

UP THE MARKET

I absolutely loved living in Chatsworth Road right on top of the very lively noisy bustling market, not only was it convenient but it provided us with hours of enjoyment and entertainment and, unlike the despicable David, I could show my face into any shop.

Markets, in those days, were the place to get bargains, and they flourished all over London. Some were small, just half a dozen stalls tucked into a tiny side street and some were vast, so vast that they covered large districts, like the famous Petticoat Lane. But none of these felt as comfortable to us locals as our dear old Chats. I suppose it was because most of the traders knew us and our families. I was often told to 'Say Hello to your mum and dad'. When our first son was born we proudly pushed him through the market and many of the traders and local people congratulated us and asked to see the new baby and to coo over him and to place a coin into the tiny hand along with the blessing of 'May you never want', an old cockney/Jewish custom. We felt so proud and pleased.

The twice-weekly market was always packed and extremely vibrant, always something to see and experience. In those days stallholders called out to the crowds to attract more trade to their stalls, these calls that were repeated all day took a life of their own almost becoming simple 'songs'. "Fresh Spanish Oranges, straight off of the boat. Come and taste 'em Muvver" was the sort of call that must have been used for hundreds of years. Sometimes a passing customer would reply, nearly always with a tongue in cheek put-down, "Come and taste 'em? If you touched 'em he would call the bleedin' Cops". This was called Cockney humour, sometimes known as backchat. One bloke who sold tinned food would brag that they had one or two dents in them 'Because they fell orf the back of a lorry'.

There must have been half a dozen Fruit and Veg. stalls dotted throughout the market. The vegetable stalls were simply piles of potatoes thrown haphazardly and sacks of onions, carrots and cabbages placed in front of them but what they lacked in visual beauty they made up with the earthy, country smells that wafted from 'freshly gathered' farm products. It was like having a day out in the country without the bother of buses and trains.

The fruit stalls were a completely different thing. The smells were more exotic, causing your imagination to take you to more tropical parts of the world, and the displays of fruit should have been featured in an art gallery. Each fruit merchant took a pride in the appearance of the display, known to them as a 'flash', and spent a lot of time creating eye-catching patterns of the season's offerings. Oranges especially were laid out in symmetrical patterns with the bright orange of the unwrapped fruit contrasting with the exquisitely wrapped ones, the wrappings making the already tasty looking fruit look much more expensive and something that you just had to taste. These flimsy paper orange wrappers had wonderfully colourful artwork on them, and became very collectable, I had a collection of the better examples that I kept in a scrap book and looking back I reckon it was them that gave me my love of lettering and display. The boxes of dates really fired my imagination with their views of desert sand dunes, palm trees, camels and nomadic tribesmen on magnificent Arabic steeds. The lettering was very 'middle eastern', and I studied it just to see what exactly made it look that way. With bunches of ripe bananas hung from the top of stall and grapes, coconuts and apples and pears crammed into to edges of the whole tableau, these stalls made the market a pleasure to stroll through.

Now you can't say that I didn't warn you that I was a world class gas bag and I did mention that I had an overcrowded brain full of information, so please don't fall asleep while I give you an example of my affliction. I mentioned that the colourful display on the stalls and shops was called a 'flash', well this name has cockney street trader origins. In Victorian times when markets were everywhere it was the fashion for men to wear black waistcoats with white pearl buttons. The many Costermongers embraced this fashion and, being the outgoing hard working type, just had to take one extra step towards extravagant dress by sewing extra buttons on the peaks of their caps and down the legs of their trousers. All the barrows and stalls were lit by bright oil lamps and the pearl buttons 'flashed' in the light encouraged by exaggerated movements, so anyone who showed off was said to be 'flash' and individuals were called 'Flash Harry'. It also was the origin of Pearly Kings and Queens.

Poverty was rife in East London and many working class areas, so, many people had to revert to scavenging for discarded food. At the end of a day's trading lots of people gathered in the markets, including Chats, and searched through the discarded foodstuff, particularly the fruit and veg. stalls. Apples, pears and similar fruits that had been bruised or damaged were gleaned and the rotten parts cut off and discarded or taken home to feed to backyard fowls. Even spuds and cabbages got the same treatment. Bacon bones and fish heads were included, but pig's trotters became a delicacy and had to be paid for. This early form of recycling continued right into the 1970s or later when supermarkets simply dumped this precious source of nutrition and renamed this practice as stealing. Now politically green groups are quite rightly discouraging this terrible waste.

A lot of the traders were very persuasive but none of the stallholders who had the gift of the gab could compete with the racing tipsters who visited the market and simply stood on the pavement selling rolled up slips of paper that had the name of the 'big winner' scrawled on them. Their schpiel was so convincing that the punters couldn't wait to slip them the 'couple of bob' to be let in on the secret. One of these very gifted talkers would dress in full racing colours, complete with polished riding boots, a silk cap and a riding crop that he used to gesticulate his well thought-out story. He would call the crowd in close to him, lower his voice, and tell of how he was in Newmarket 'last night' and was privy to a juicy bit of information. With a serious look upon his face and one eye looking out for a copper he suggested that a certain race had been fixed and, simply by the goodness of his heart, he was going to share his good fortune with half of London. "This horse can't lose" he assured, and just to emphasise the fact he crouched to a racing position and used his crop to whip some imaginary steed.

Now and then we were privileged to have the 'World Famous' Prince Monolulu, come to Chatsworth Road. This flamboyant and very entertaining racing tipster brought his own charismatic performance with him. Well, he really was quite famous, he could be seen at all the big race meetings and events, even rubbing shoulders with royalty and film stars, so it was a thrill to see him in our own market. His full title was 'Ras Prince Monolulu' and in spite of this obvious made-up name he claimed to be an Ethiopian Prince and just to prove it dressed in almost pantomime outfits. His long, flowing, colourful robes were decorated with bangles and necklaces and topped with an elaborate head dress complete with tall ostrich feathers. It was impossible to miss him in a crowd, but he made doubly sure by calling loudly his very familiar call "I gotta horse, I gotta horse". He delighted the crowds by talking drivel, he just had to light up the street with his wide smile and shout whatever he wanted to and everyone would be delighted. I once heard him calling "I gotta horse, roast beef and three veg!" Absolute drivel, but delivered in such an enjoyable manner. There is an old superstition that says a tall dark stranger will bring you luck, well Prince Monolulu cashed in on this belief by inviting punters to 'Touch a black man for luck'. This was common practice for many years, and I do believe that it him that started the questionable practice.

It was boasted that you could buy anything 'Up Chats' and it was no false claim. Every thing from High Fashion to cat's meat could be found. Rosemans the tailors made top quality suits for both men and women, Pearl Stewart supplied the latest fashionable women's wear and added a bit of chic to the area, and Lou's sock shop supplied shirts, socks, underwear, and kindness. Lou, who everyone called Alf, was a short, happy, Jewish bloke who ran the shop with his wife and son and earned the love of all his customers. One example of his warmth and decency was when one day my wife went in to buy some trousers for our small son. "I am not sure which ones that I like or if they will fit him" she told Alf, "he is not well indoors and I can't bring him out". Alf gathered a selection of trousers and placed them into my wife's bag and said "Take them home and sort out a pair for the little lad then bring the others back, I wish him well". That was Alf, a real kind gent!

   To cope with people's dietary needs there were at least six butchers shops and a very well stocked 'Home and Colonial Stores'. The butchers all did a roaring trade, each one making their own sausages, black puddings and pates and bragging that their products were the best in the market. Because of the competition each shop put on a very enticing window display, prime cuts, chops and 'livers and lights' were laid out in an artistic fashion, each display centred by a real pig's head complete with apples and oranges adorning it. Outside poultry was hung in vertical rows, a lot of them unplucked and placed next to rabbits still in their furry skins. As a kid I was enchanted by the china figures of cute, woolly lambs that decorated the shelves, I wanted my mum to buy one but it never happened. Every shop's floor was thickly sprinkled with sawdust that gave the premises a fresh smell of timber, I can smell it now.

   On the corner of Elderfield Road, just out of the Market was a shop simply called 'Primmy's'. Primmy, whose full name was Primrose, sold 'Shop Soiled' ladies footwear. Every Saturday morning Primmy arrived with a van load of 'straight off of the catwalk' latest fashion shoes. An excited crowd of shoe seekers filled the pavement awaiting the opening time and when the canny Primmy pushed the doors open there would be a near stampede of bargain hunters with their hands full of ready cash.

During the 1960s there were still a lot of old fashioned businesses plying their trade, they sound a little archaic now. For instance there was a corn chandler, an oil shop, a hardware shop, two knitting wool shops, a gent's outfitters and a couple of traditional grocer's shops. The wool shops were a joy to go into, all French polished interior and lots of soft, cosy looking wool packed into the many compartments that lined the walls, what's more you were served by nice old ladies who must have been made especially to work in such clean and peaceful outlets.

The old fashioned grocery shops had large counters down each side, one of them held a marble slab where the cooked meats were sliced. In front of these counters were large tins of biscuits with glass lids and when you asked for them the biscuits were taken out and put into a crisp brown paper bag and then weighed. We often had the cheapest ones, the broken biscuits, they held the promise of finding a big bit, if you were lucky. They may have been cheap but the tasted good to us.

Entering the corn chandler's shop was like travelling back in time, the plain floor boards creaked and amplified your footsteps as you walked around the many bins of seeds and fertilisers. The inside seemed much darker than the bright day outside and there was a comforting smell of hay, the owner, who was a nice but almost silent man gave the place a slight trace of mystery. On the shelves were rows of boxes that contained products to make your fowls lay bigger eggs, to kill pests, and some more to make your canary even more yellow and to sing sweeter. I was strangely fascinated by these remedies from a bygone age.

Perhaps the most loved and best remembered shop was Arthur Tom's Pie and Mash Shop. With its traditional pie-shop interior complete with sawdust on the floor and its display of live eels wriggling in a metal tray on the pavement outside, it was a magnet for all local food lovers old and young. Just two doors away from the pie shop was the local undertaker's workshop. The close proximity of the two businesses gave rise to rumours of a connecting tunnel, but these thoughts never stopped anyone from scoffing the delicious delicacy pies and mash. The lady who served behind the counter was short and very fat. She was also burdened by a most unusual medical problem, she had a very swollen neck that made her look like she was looking at you from the middle of an inflated inner tube. Some kids simply laughed at her strange appearance, some were absolutely horrified by it, but me, I was fascinated by it and stared at her so much that my mum would grab me by the hand and drag me out of the shop where she told me that I should pity the poor unfortunate woman and not to do it again.

No kid could pass the nearby Chemist shop without pestering its mum for a glass of the darkly delicious Sarsaparilla that was dispensed from an oak barrel temptingly placed on a table outside of the pharmacy. This shop, that was next to Ada's newspaper shop, was the first one in the market to have an Asian owner. He was young, very friendly, well-spoken and smart. He would greet all his customers into the pharmacy with a huge smile that displayed his massive set of sparkling white teeth, what's more he continued to sell the market's favourite drink.

From time to time the market-goers were treated to an impromptu event when someone, usually a trader, had a difference of opinion with a punter. The customary backchat became just a bit more heated and, if we were lucky, a full scale 'Bull and a Cow' (row) would break out. Voices were raised, put-downs grew into insults and sometimes a swearing contest was held, all to the enjoyment of the rubber-necking crowds. At a certain time one of the onlookers would get annoyed, poke his nose in and offer their opinion only to be challenged by someone else on the pavement, now things got interesting and threats were issued, but I can honestly say that these free entertainments never erupted into violence.

When things got a bit tedious and there was nothing on the Telly, me and my wife would switch on Chats's own Channel and open our window and sit and watch the world and a bit of Hackney pass by. We were quite well known, so some passers-by would stop and have a pavement to first floor chat, and in those days many people unknown to us just passed the time of day with us. We were never short of sights to be seen, nearly every evening a bargee would pass with his barge horse on their way to a stable, this man who wore one of those working man's caps that looked like it had been moulded to his head rode side-saddle on the back of the slow-walking, placid beast. I took a photo of this rustic scene but it seems to have been lost in the passing of time.

Late at night the very spooky Janey Pepperhole would push her home-made barrow up the hill as she returned from a days trading selling seafood outside the Prince of Wales at Lea Bridge. As she squeaked her barrow past our flat the bright Tilley lamp on her stall swung backwards and forwards lighting up our bedroom with each swing.

One of the things that I enjoyed was the now defunct pastime of singing in the street, I was brought up listening to boozers leaving the pub singing their way home, sometimes in tune, sometimes in harmony. This pleasing tradition still went on and I got pleasure from hearing the music drifting up to our flat. I believe that The Beatles were the last composers to write music that could be sung in the streets, and the proof of this statement was me hearing young girls warbling Lennon and McCartney songs as they walked late at night down Chatsworth Road, followed by a very inebriated Frank the Barber having a loud argument with himself as he tried to work out what shop was his. Never a dull moment in Chats!

No account of Chatsworth Road Market would be complete if I didn't mention Reg. Mother Nature had not been kind to Reg, he was very deaf, needing two hearing aids, he dribbled a lot and his large clumsy feet caused him to clomp along awkwardly.

Nevertheless he was an integral part of the market and the area. He was big bloke, as strong as an ox and had bags of energy. He, I believe, worked for himself and pulled most of the stalls out and put them in the appropriate place when market day came. Most of the small backyards and alleyways housed the many stalls and it was no mean feat to do this arduous job and to run errands and help the stall holders, but Reg just plodded on in his own way. A lot of the traders who made a good living in Chats owed a deep debt to him. In the evenings you could find him in local pubs, not drinking but working as a Potman, he never stopped working! Of course it was rumoured that Reg had many biscuit tins stuffed with banknotes hidden away under his floor boards. Who knows?

DUCKING AND DIVING!

The noble art, or perhaps I should say ignoble art, of ducking and diving must have been in existence for hundreds of years and many a fine tale, fictitious or true has been told about it, so why should I be left out?

My introduction to this way of 'getting by', 'making ends meet' 'putting food on the table' etc. was at a very early age when the war was at its height and things were scarce.

Buying food off of the ration book or from under the counter was common practice and if you bought anything from the black market it seemed to taste better. The one hard and fast, unbreakable rule was – don't ask where it came from.

When I was about 12 years old my dad was working outside of London somewhere, he came home one night with a much prized article under his arm, something that had never been seen before, something that would raise our status in the neighbourhood and set us apart from 'ordinary' people. It was a… plastic toilet seat! What is more it was white and what is even more it had a lid on it. Mum could not take her eyes off of it while Dad fitted it, she was so proud that she immediately called all the neighbours in to show it off to them. Before this toilet seats were made of wood that had to be varnished every year, sometimes causing your bum to get stuck to it. They were always dark brown and a bit unhealthy looking, but this one that must have come from Hollywood because it lit up our tiny lav. Of course everyone for miles around wanted one and Dad never let them down, resulting in the deal being a nice little earner and the outhouses of Lea Bridge moving an inch or two nearer to Buckingham Palace.

Many people were offered goods that had 'fallen off the back of a lorry' by 'a bloke that they had met in a pub' and if you wanted anything specific you put the word out and a friend of a friend would come up with the goods, so it was possible to earn a living at ducking and diving without the inconvenience of working.

I worked in a big factory with access to lots of workers, all potential punters, and fancied myself as a bit of a wheeler-dealer, so if anything worthwhile was offered I would snap it up. One quiet Sunday evening we were sitting watching TV, on the telly was a newcomer, a very promising young bloke called Bruce Forsyth, his performance was interrupted by a ring on the doorbell. Standing in the alley was a friend of a friend of mine with a box under his arm. He opened the box to reveal a classy looking pair of shoes, grey winkle-pickers they were, all the rage at the time. "Can you shift some of these?" he asked. I tried to hide my eagerness as we struck a bargain. "How many have you got?" said I, "Not many" was the short reply. With an air of cockiness I waved my arm in the direction of the narrow stairs and said "Fetch them up!" Upstairs we looked out of the window to see a small lorry that had a bit of damage to the back of it and my newly acquired mate and his helper loading themselves up with shoe boxes and struggling up the stairs. Then they did it again, and then again. "Just how many have you got?" I nervously asked, "Nearly finished" he said unconvincingly. At last they were unloaded and both scarpered sharply with a "See you on Friday"

Poor old Brucie was completely forgotten as we viewed our tiny flat that now resembled a stockroom, we stacked the boxes as neatly as we could up the walls, behind and on top of the wardrobes, under the bed, in fact in any available space. My cockiness took a tumble as I thought to myself "Oh dear, I think that I have bitten off more that I can chew". We went to bed that night with a feeling of unease in our stomachs, the smell of cardboard boxes in our noses and the sound of creaking boxes in our ears, not the most comfortable of nights.

The next day at the factory the punters were fighting to order these stylish and rather stupid looking shoes, and by Wednesday they were all gone and paid for, what a relief! All that was left of the mountain of footwear was a dozen or so single shoes that I carelessly tossed into our outside toilet. I paid the supplier and retained my cockiness. All was well, but not for too long, because on Saturday evening we were relaxing in front of the telly when one of those 'Keep Your Eyes Peeled' police shows came on and flashing across the screen was a beautiful pair of grey winkle-pickers and an appeal to call the Old Bill if you happened to be offered any of them. The feeling of unease returned to our stomachs and not without good cause because it seems that a couple of villains had backed a lorry through the front of a shop and cleared the stock. That was probably the only time that I questioned the time-honoured, unwritten law of not asking where the goods came from.

When my first son was born in the Hackney Hospital it was customary for the mums to be confined to the maternity ward for a week or more, so I was on my own for the first time. A bloke asked me if I wanted any shirts. I took a look at them. They looked very special because they were packed in a box with a cellophane lid, a rare thing then. He was asking ten bob a piece for them and I knew that I could get a pound a lump with no trouble, so I bought a load of them and put them into my van to take to the factory. In the factory the women almost fought each other to get their sticky hands on them and at going home time I only had six shirts left.

That night I visited my wife and our newborn miracle of life. I was feeling so good that instead of going home to an empty flat I took a little drive around the area just to show off. I was making my way home along a road near to Victoria Park when a large figure waving a torch stepped into the road, it was of course a copper. "Good Evening sir" he boomed, "Just a routine check, is this your vehicle?" "Can you tell me the registration number?" I answered with confidence and a little bit of that cockiness when I suddenly remembered the Dicky Dirts in the back of the van. "What is the purpose of your journey?" he asked, "I'm just going home" I mumbled, "What is in the back?. I held my breath as I opened the doors and the rays of his torch fell upon the offending shirts, he didn't quite say "Hello, hello, hello, what's all this then?" but his manner had now changed from the routine one that he started with to a more investigative one. "Are they your shirts?" he said, "Yes" I croaked. "You've got a lot" he said with suspicion. "Yes" I stammered. "My wife is in hospital for a week and I can't do washing so I bought myself enough clean shirts to last me for a week." He now lost interest in the shirts and asked "What is your wife in hospital for?" "She has just had a baby" said I with just a bit of pride. "Oh yeah, what did she have?" I told him that it was a boy and our first child. A smile came to his face and he proudly proclaimed "We have just had a baby boy and it is our firstborn". Then he thrust a leather gloved hand into mine and said "Congratulations".

I returned his good wishes and drove home before he had a chance to show me photos of his pride and joy.

DUCKING AND DIVING!

Of course when taking part in such clandestine dealing it is advisable to take everything that is said to you with a large pinch of salt. There is a very old myth that there is 'Honour amongst thieves', well don't believe it for one minute. I always approached every offer with disbelief, if it seemed too good to be true then that's exactly what it was. I never listened to any strangers who slipped up to me in a pub or a market and presented me with the bargain of a lifetime.

This is where the 'friend of a friend' network came in handy. Somehow it was a bit more trustworthy if a familiar name was mentioned. But not always. When one of my mates was offered the latest record playing sound system at a give-away price, he gladly handed over the cash and was delighted with what he was given. "Have you got any more?" he asked. "Yeah, I've got a couple of dozen" replied the unknown punter. "My mates would like some, I am sure". "Well, take the order and meet me at that big pub in Bethnal Green tomorrow" was the answer. My trusting mate took the record player around to his work mates and got eight orders, with the workmates handing him the cash with the expected pleasure of owning the latest bit of audio kit. The following evening my mate called into the pub and there was his supplier sitting at a table. "Sit down and have a drink" he convivially said. "Have you got the money?" Our trusting mate patted his pocket and nodded his head, "Don't get it out here, let's go into the toilet".

Already alarm bells are ringing in your heads, what a pity they never rang in the right head. Inside the bog the money was handed over and meticulously counted, the supplier tucked the money safely away and said "Thanks for the cash" and shook my mate by the hand, but his other hand swung round and landed a vicious blow right on the poor sod's nose, knocking him to the floor. As he recovered his senses he just glimpsed the back of the slippery, light-footed geyser disappearing through the door.

I could tell you at least half a dozen similar tales, so I never trusted anyone on face value. During my lorry driving days I was approached by a very iffy bloke about six or seven times over a period of ten years or so. I wouldn't even talk much to him because things just did not add up about him. For a start he did not look right, he was an older man who looked like someone from an old black and white film. It was the way he dressed that gave him this look. He wore a well-worn flat cap and a brown warehouse coat. I mean, who wore these outdated overalls and where would you find them if you wanted to wear them? He said that he was a van driver but there was never the sight of a van, and he always asked if I knew anyone who could shift any 'goods', then he would rattle off a list of the most unusual mixture of groceries, drinks, cigarettes and, mysteriously, Luncheon Meat! I simply acted too busy to talk to him, something strange was going on and I did not want to go anywhere near it. Mind you, my curiosity nearly got the better of me.

This caution about dodgy dealings came about because I had been taken in by some smooth-talking fly-by-night merchants when I was still wet behind the ears. I must have been aged nine or ten and was in the habit of going to Petticoat Lane every Sunday. The Lane in those days was a mass of heaving humanity and full of every fiddler, tea leaf, trickster and ne'er-do-well that could be found in London. At that time the luxury that no-one could get their hands on was Nylon stockings (Blimey, that dates it), but there, smack in the middle of the market was a stall piled with boxes with pictures of beautiful nylon clad legs on them, pinned all around the stall were cellophane packets with similar pictures.

Crowds pressed around the stall as the schmoozer started his patter. These very expensive hosiery items were being offered at a stupidly low price, the crowd pushed forward even harder to reach the luxurious, glamorous articles that had been delicately displayed by the very smooth talking barker. I couldn't wait to hand over my two and a tanner and get a brown paper bag full of stockings shoved ungraciously into my hand.

All the way home I held tight onto my special gift for my dear Mum. I was so pleased with myself and knew that my mum would be moved to tears by my loving gesture.

When I arrived home reality hit me right between the eyes. When mum shook the 'stockings' out of the bag, there was not one perfect stocking to be seen. Instead there was a pile of damaged, half finished, mis-matched items that I guess were the contents of the waste bin in the stocking factory. Mum did shed tears that day, not tears of joy but tears of laughter that rolled down her cheeks as she held up the forlorn pieces of schmatter. I had learned a lesson the hard way, one that I never forgot. I bet that most East End kids could tell a similar story.

VOTE FOR TED

My little backyard menagerie grew with pigeons, rabbits, birds and even lizards living comfortably with each other and at the same time my family grew, making our cosy little flat not quite as comfortable as it should be. As a result we were offered new accommodation on the still being built Clapton Park, I had asked for somewhere that would suit my peculiar needs and was assured that it would be done. I was immediately offered a flat on the third floor, nice view but no garden. Of course I refused it, but was soon allotted another with a fair sized garden. At the viewing I asked about my mini-zoo and the very convivial man who was conducting the proceedings smiled widely and assured me that I could keep what I wanted in my garden, "That's what a garden is for" said he.

Anticipating the move I had got rid of all of my livestock except for the kid's favourite bunny 'Fredrica', who lived in a highly decorated hutch which was placed in the almost bare garden. Within a week of moving in the Housing Manager knocked at our door demanding to examine our garden, his face dropped when he saw Fredrica and her lovely little home, "That's an illegal structure" he said and to underline it he issued us with an eviction notice. "And no animals are allowed" he added. I was not pleased!

Now let me tell you that I have always been a cantankerous, argumentative bloke when the situation called for it and my years spent as a shop steward had given me an acute sense of injustice. I was ready to put this right this diabolical wrong.

Believe it or not but at that time the Tories were in power in Hackney, so I wrote to my local councillor, a Tory, asking him to see me about a matter that was very important to me. I was not going to let on that I wanted to talk about a rabbit, but rabbit or not he never replied so I wrote to him again along with three other Tory councillors, but still not so much as a rattle of the letter-box. With great confidence in working class solidarity I wrote to three Labour councillors who adopted the same disrespectful attitude as the other party. I even wrote to our local Communist councillor to no avail so there was nothing else that I could do but go to the main man. I wrote to the Prime Minister, Mr. Ted Heath!

I complained that his councillors were ignoring the very people who had voted them in.

"Is this Tory policy?" I asked, feeling very hard done by.

I honestly thought that I would not get a reply but, to my surprise and excitement, within a week or so a very nice crisp envelope with a very nice Portcullis embossed on it dropped through our letter-box. The letter, written on high quality paper that even smelled expensive, had the same heavily embossed House of Commons logo on it. I felt just a little nervous. It was from Ted Heath's secretary and said that "Mr. Heath is aware of your concern and will see that any problems that you have will be listened to". It was not exactly permission to install a zoological gardens in my backyard, but it was a step in the right direction.

The following Sunday was a bright and sunny day. My kids were playing peacefully, the dinner was cooking filling the kitchen with a pleasant smell, the whole place was a picture of domestic bliss when there was a knock on the door. I opened the door and there stood an immaculate man looking like he had just stepped out of Burton's window. He wore a very expensive, well-cut suit and one of those blue shirts with a white collar that made him look like someone important. A silk tie with matching pocket handkerchief and a fresh cut yellow rose on his lapel finished off his well thought out ensemble. I was impressed. He smiled at me and asked "Mr. Walker?" "Yes" I said. "The Prime Minister has asked me to come to see you" said he smiling even wider. I hesitated for a moment while I tried to take in the last statement and then stammered "do come in". I led him into the front room and sat him in a comfortable chair, he complimented us on our 'very nice room' and we complimented him on his tasteful dress sense, tea was served in our best china and a plateful of assorted biscuits were offered and accepted, we were all enjoying this very civilised visit. I then relayed to him my sorrowful story of being ignored by all the local politicians of all shades and he sympathised with me adding that Mr. Heath is a very nice man and cares about everyone in the country. I was not in a position to argue.

We finished the small talk along with the assorted biscuits so it was time for business. Our stylish visitor took on a more serious manner as he asked "Now what is this matter that means so much to you and that you want to discuss?" I led him to the garden and to the rabbit hutch and a very disinterested Fredrica. "There it is" I said. "They want to evict me because of this after I was promised that I could keep it". Well, fair play to him, he did a very good job of hiding his disappointment. He waved his hand in the direction of the troublesome hutch, said "I will have a word with the appropriate people" and very politely made his exit.

Later that week I received a letter from the Housing Officer saying that I could now keep the rabbit but only until it died and then I was not to replace it. This was not exactly the news that I wanted to hear so in keeping with my anti-establishment ideals I tore it up, ignored the contents and carried on doing whatever I wanted to! After all, I had my mate Ted Heath on my side.

NEVER JUDGE A BOOK BY ITS COVER

Just yesterday I went on my usual morning walk. As I walked to the river bank I passed our local bus stop, slumping on the uncomfortable seat was a black bloke who I guess was in his late thirties. He had the hood of his jacket pulled up, he needed a shave and his scowling face looked uncared for and weary. He was puffing on a very large fag so I felt just a bit uncomfortable and wary.

In spite of this I gave him my customary "Morning Mate". He looked up and replied "Hello, how are you? How are you keeping?" I was not sure if he knew me or if I knew him but now felt more comfortable with him so I stopped and said that I was well and still living in the area and asked him if he was well. I also asked him "Where are you living now?" "Not 'round here" he said. "I am just visiting my mum", as he waved his hand in the direction of a block of houses. It seemed so easy to say "How is your mum?" His face never changed as he said "She is a lot better now, Fanks" and then said "She has had a little bit of breast cancer, but her hair is growing back now, I'm keeping my eye on her". It just seemed so natural to say "I'm glad, give her my love". "I will do that Uncle" he said. Uncle is a term of respect for an older man and it made me feel warm towards this shabby stranger. "See you later" I said, and he thrust out a fist for me to touch with mine just like the young black kids do. I returned the fist salute and went on my way feeling good.

I DON'T BELIEVE IN GHOSTS!

Yes, you heard me right. I Do Not Believe in Ghosts nor fairies, angels, spirits, ancestors looking down on me from some celestial cloud and definitely not in Gods of any kind. Now that we are clear about this I can start this story.

The events in this tale took place on the first night of our occupation of our new home on Clapton Park. The previous day or two had been spent shifting our furniture and belongings from our old flat in Chatsworth Road into the bare rooms of our spanking brand new maisonette that was situated in the middle of a building site and demolition area and was one of the earliest blocks to be habitable. What's more, only a handful of the maisonettes were occupied, none of this worried us because we had bedrooms, a bathroom and central heating and were excited about our future in these almost palatial surroundings.

Almost everything that we owned was packed in cardboard boxes and plonked in various rooms with no form of organisation and each movement of our chattels echoed around the bare walls. I could not stand the drabness of the untreated plaster so decided to splash a bit of coloured paint in as many rooms as I could and to this end bought half a dozen tins of decorators emulsion. The floors were all finished in very nice tiles so I placed a few sheets of brown wrapping paper on the floor and placed the paint tins on them to protect the shiny gloss finish of the sparkling, ice rink-like floors.

We went to bed that night with a mixture of apprehension and excitement and just a little concern about our three very young sons who had never slept in their own room before. Well, the excitement and concern were outweighed by the long day of lifting and shifting and we all fell into a deep sleep within minutes snuggled up in between the unpacked cases.

I DON'T BELIEVE IN GHOSTS!

In the middle of the night something disturbed me and I sat up in bed thinking that the kids had somehow got out of bed, I went into their room to see them spark out and looking like three little cherubs. I returned to my bed, my wife slept on unaware of my nocturnal wanderings, I decided that all was well and that I had imagined the something that I thought that I had heard, when there it was again! It was no imagination, it was clearly the sound of someone rustling the brown wrapping paper and dragging the paper and the paint across the floor. My stomach turned as I realised that someone was in our home so I adopted the very British practice of putting the sheet over my head and shaking like a leaf. The noise happened again now causing my poor old stomach to tie itself in knots and make my knees knock, it was then that my wife woke and asked me "What is the matter?" Putting my bravest face on I said "Nothing, I just thought that the kids had woken up". Just as she closed her eyes to resume her beauty sleep, the noise sounded again, "Oh!" she said, or words to that effect, "there is someone downstairs dragging the paint across the floor". Well, Thank You very much Mrs. Walker for confirming my suspicions just when I had convinced myself that it was only a freak wind blowing under the door. "What are you going to do?" she said from the relative safety of her bed. "Go downstairs and see what's going on". "What me, go down on my own?" I thought. "Never!"

I pulled myself up to my full height and told myself "Now come on Brian, you have been in the Army". Then I reasoned that in the Army I had two things to help me be brave, a loaded rifle and a regiment of British Squaddies to back me up. Where were they now that I needed them?

Nevertheless my sense of protection of my kids and the thought of looking cowardly in front of my wife overcame my fear just enough to convince me to descend the stairs, but not unarmed I thought. I am in the habit of sleeping naked so, not wanting to be cruel to the intruder, I slipped on a pair of Y-Fronts and opened one of the many packing cases to find something to arm myself with. Inside the first case was a set of glass balls in a string netting, they were fishermen's floats that we had bought on one of our holidays to the West Country, they had never been floated in the sea but now they were to be used to bash someone's brains in. I shakily moved down the stairs with some fisherman's balls in one hand and my other hand protecting something similar of my own. The sweat ran down my bare back as I reached the foot of the stairs and burst into the kitchen swinging the glass orbs as threateningly as I could. Phew, no-one there. Now for the living room so, with teeth glaring and bare chest stuck out, I crashed the door open with a kick that John Wayne would have been proud of. Phew again, not a soul there. So now I was full of bravado and denying that I was ever afraid when it occurred to me that there was a small toilet near the front door. The sweat appeared again as I just knew that the crafty trespasser was crouching in the smallest room. Time for another swing of the balls and this time I heard myself grunting a war cry, all to an empty bog.

 I returned to bed like a warrior returning from battle and feeling so manly when suddenly the noise of the moving paint tins echoed around the house again, I checked the tins but they had not moved, not even a fraction of an inch. My wife was petrified but I knew that nothing was downstairs that could harm us, after all I don't believe in ghosts. The sound continued through the night so we had plenty of opportunities to analyze it so I can positively say that some unexplained force was 'moving' the paint tins. I was getting a little bored with the busy 'poltergeist' and drifted off to sleep only to be woken by my frantic wife screaming "It's coming up the stairs!!!!" Sure enough the frightening sound of footsteps on the bare uncarpeted stairs could be heard. When they reached the top of the stairs thankfully they stopped, then silence at last.

 We made enquiries about any intruders or noisy heating

appliances but everyone we spoke to gave us a knowing look and in their minds tapped their temples. We have never been troubled since. We have never been able to give a satisfactory explanation for that strange and frightening night.

There is a postscript to this tale that was even more scary but can be explained. About six months later, when we were settled in to our new home and all the walls were painted and the shock of that strange night had subsided, we were sleeping soundly in our cosy bed when a deafening crash woke us and made us seem to jump as high as the ceiling. Our hearts were beating fit to burst out of our chests. As we sat shaking on the edge of the bed we saw that a big oval mirror in our dressing table had fallen out striking a glass shelf causing the terrifying sound and awakening our memories of that spooky night. I had never felt so scared in my life. All I could think of was that ghosts don't like to see themselves in a mirror so had tried to break it. The thought of this filled me with fear and anxiety, but that is stupid, – after all I don't believe in ghosts!

The truth is that the mirror had been displaced by the central heating drying out the glue that held it in place. Or could it be something from some paranormal world, you know, one of those that I don't believe in?

THE ANOINTING

After the trauma of our unwanted visitor on the very first night in our new home we settled down to meet the more earthly neighbours who began trickling in to the new block. This block stood in the middle of a building site. There were no pavements, railings or footpaths, just mud, trenches with scaffolding boards across them and more mud. All the old houses that were now empty still stood in all the surrounding streets, giving the whole area a feeling of despair and isolation, so the appearance of almost anyone was welcome. As the weeks went by most of the flats began being occupied and people being people everyone was scrutinised with a mixture of curiosity and concern.

"Supposing we don't get on together" was a question asked many times, "I do hope we don't get a wrong'un living next door" was on every mind. This was at a time when minorities tended to live together in their own areas, but the letting officers never took any notice of your colour or culture so us newcomers found ourselves living in close quarters to tenants from many parts of the world for the first time. Of course, suspicions and awkwardness made us act very tentatively around each other, but we found that a good old fashioned introduction and a handshake made the suspicions melt away and be replaced by curiosity, and made us realise that everyone was the same.

It was summer, and the heatwave couldn't have come at a better time. Most of us came out to sit on the communal balconies to get the benefit of the cool air and within a few days we all knew all the details and even some of the gossip of what was rapidly becoming a new community. Friendships soon formed and some of the families eventually became close, there are a handful of these pioneer families still living here.

THE ANOINTING

One of the families became very close to me almost immediately in a way that I would not have chosen.

The family, the Abiyomes, consisted of dad Tunji, his wife Vera and their two young daughters. We had passed social niceties between us but thanks to the sloppy builders of the block we were thrust into the closest of relationships whether we wanted it or not. The peace of the tropical afternoon was violently disturbed by one of the young daughters screaming at the top of her voice and by her dad Tunji roaring and slamming a door. The two girls continued the frantic screaming as they ran out onto the balcony, but Tunji remained completely silent as he cowered behind the kitchen door. Vera stood on a chair in the front room, her face contorting with horror and disgust. What put them all into a panic was not some vicious creature or impending disaster but a blockage in the toilet that caused a liberal amount of the people upstairs' waste product to flood the Abiyome's ground floor. Now let's not beat about the bush, the waste product was what we in Hackney call SHIT, come to think of it, that name is used all over the world. Tunji by now was nearly passing out because he was covering his nose and mouth with his handkerchief and rather stupidly forgetting to breathe, so the girls called to me, a relative stranger, to do something. I stuck my nose into the front door and in my cocky East End manner simply said "It's only shit, why are you panicking?" "Yyyyuchhh!" cried Tunji from behind his barricaded kitchen door. I took that as meaning "I am not coming out!" Vera was still on her chair, the girls were being comforted by sympathetic onlookers and I just casually went to get my shovel and yard broom. Just like my hero, Corporal Jones, I told them not to panic as I shovelled shit and threw copious amounts of disinfectant about the ground floor. When I was finished and fresh air and Izal disinfectant dominated the area, Tunji nervously ventured from his bunker to thank me by throwing his arms around me and kissing me forcefully on both cheeks, the two girls stopped crying and Vera gently descended from the chair. The blockage was caused by the workers who plastered the walls throwing the waste plaster down the bog. I bet they didn't know what a stink they would kick up and that they would cement a friendship ... perhaps cement was not a good choice of words.

Tunji was a Nigerian and Vera was a local girl from an old established East End family, she met Tunji when she was 16 and immediately fell for his considerable charms. They married after a short courtship and stayed together until Tunji died. They married in the mid 50s at a time when mixed marriages were frowned upon. I always considered them to be extremely brave.

NIGERIAN KNEES-UP

The very likable Tunji was a handsome, articulate, charismatic man with a fine style of dressing. He was proud of his African status, he always wore traditional Nigerian garb, tasteful, colourful kaftan-like robes, carefully fitted narrow bottomed trousers and some times a natty hat, his dark face was marked by tribal scars and most times had a huge smile on it. Whenever he met you he would enthusiastically greet you with a very physical hug and a noisy greeting, he would laugh at the silliest of jokes.

He was, I suppose, middle class with a large circle of influential Nigerian friends. These friends frequently visited him and Vera and were forever keen to party. The men were smartly dressed in expensive suits and the women wore wonderfully colourful African dresses, they finished off the ensemble with a brilliant display of jewellery that glittered with every movement of their voluptuous bodies. One of the men, known to us as 'The Major' was in fact an officer in the Nigerian Army and certainly looked the part with a well tailored blazer with regimental badge on the pocket and a regimental tie with his crisp white shirt, he even had a British Army officers moustache, brushed to part in the middle and spread across his benevolent face.

Tunji's very amiable circle of friends were regular visitors and before too long the party that they craved was organised. Vera and Tunji asked all the neighbours in but only a few turned up. Of course I, the hero of the shit and shovel brigade, was commanded to attend and not to disappoint turned up with my wife and my Mum and Dad. We were all greeted like royalty, everyone lining up to shake hands with us. Mum and Dad were kissed by all the guests, and a lot of the twinkling, voluptuous ladies hugged my Dad and told him what a fine looking fellow he was. He beamed like a lighthouse. We were shepherded to the big armchair where 'The Major' had settled and one by one were presented to him, he offered a hand for us to shake and told us how pleased he was to meet us. The women had their hand kissed, making my Mum feeling equal to my still beaming Dad.

The drink flowed and the dancing started. The music was inviting, it was modern Nigerian music, lots of African rhythms influenced by American pop music and jazz, my dad called it 'a good bit of jump up and down music'. Soon the room was full of joyful dancers boog-a-looing and doing other current dances. It was so enjoyable but there was a drawback, the records went on for fifteen minutes or more. The Nigerian dancers took it all in their stride but us poor old Anglo-Saxons flagged after ten minutes or so.

The Major happily strode amongst the dancers, scrutinising their enthusiasm. If he spotted anyone that he thought was good he showed his appreciation by sticking a twenty pound note to their sweaty brow. I danced as hard as I could but it was my mum that was awarded the accolade when a large hand slapped a banknote on to her head. Being brought up to stand on her own two feet and not to take charity she protested and tried to hand her reward back, but the charming Major was having none of it. She reluctantly took the note but a few weeks later still had it and asked if the Major had asked for it back. He hadn't.

Food was provided and was placed on a table that was groaning under the weight of the Afro-Anglo cuisine. Lots of unidentifiable

African delicacies were placed next to jellied eels, cockles, mussels and even winkles, there was lots of exploring by both sides of guest list with surprising results. Employed to help with the catering was a lean, scrawny African man who I happily describe as a bushman, a proper native African who was unaffected by European and American culture. He and my dad were drawn to each other and apart from difficulties with heavy accents they chatted away. Dad asked him how old he was not knowing that our bushman's culture never had dates. He simply replied that "I was born when the river came this high", indicating with a rough working man's hand. Dad was thrilled and introduced him to East London food. Jellied eels were eaten with not much reaction, prawns did a bit better, but when he spied the winkles the bushman put one on his mouth still in its shell and tried to crack it with his teeth. "Hold up, you will break your bleed'n teeth!" said dad, trying his best not to laugh.

The unlikely mates chatted on and all was well until the throbbing music got into our bushman and he took to the floor. All the 'sophisticated' Nigerians danced like people of the 1970s danced all over the world, a mixture of Top of the Pops, American west coast with a touch of downtown Accra, but this stupid shaking did not impress this particular bushman. Many generations of native dancing could not be ignored and we were treated to the kind of dancing that you can only see in T.V. documentaries, arms stretching out, body bending from the waist almost making his head touch the floor. The 'sophisticated' guests acted in the most unsophisticated way and man-handled our newly acquired mate out of the front door and slammed it shut. The letterbox was pushed open and a stream of abuse flowed back into the room, all in bushman language so we were denied the pleasure of what could have been a lesson in cursing.

THE BITER BITTEN

The parties became frequent events and we were invited every time. They were marvellous but they did drain your energy, so it was time to refuse the invitation and spend a restful Saturday night in front of the Telly. At the last minute Tunje informed us that 'there will be a party tonight' and I told Vera that I would not be there. Within a minute or so there was a frantic knocking on my door. There stood a very agitated Tunji who demanded to know just why I would not be attending yet another marathon party. I came out with a feeble fib and said that "I am not feeling well". "What is the matter with you?" he demanded like some kind of inquisitor. "Erm ... I have got a bad stomach" I replied, without too much thought. Tunji disappeared immediately and I thought that he had got the message, but within a minute or two he was back with a small paper bag in his hand. Inside the bag were a dozen dried up leaves like you would find in your garden.

"Swallow some of this" he demanded. "No" I said. "They will make you feel good by clearing your stomach" he said. Pushing his face closer to mine, he glared at me and shouted "Go on!" I thought that if I did he would leave me alone so I put a crumb or two into my gob,. "More than that" he insisted and took a generous pinch of this repulsive looking herbal medicine and forced it into my closed mouth. "No" said I. "It will cure you!" he shouted back. I'm afraid his forceful nature got the better of me and with great disbelief I swallowed the vile, dry, tasteless dose of who knows what. I was annoyed with myself but at least I had got rid of him.

Any ideas that I had of settling down for a cosy night in flew out of the window with the first gripe of my stomach. I spent the rest of the evening and half of the night sitting on the lav wishing that I could die and leave my aching stomach and spinning head behind.

THE BITER BITTEN

I vowed never to pull the wool over old Tunji's eyes again.

Every now and then Tunji would float off to Nigeria for an unspecified amount of time and reappear when he felt like it. Some years ago a flight of fancy took him back to his beloved homeland and we haven't seen him since. We believe that he is dead.

Vera is still our neighbour and her young daughters are now mature women and there are grandchildren and great grandchildren. This year Vera celebrated her 80th Birthday and of course there was a party, I'm pleased to say that the many friends who came to the celebration were of many cultures and on the menu was Curry Goat and Rice and ... Jellied Eels.

A LIGHT IN THE DARK

After about a year the building site that we lived in the middle of had not progressed much but some of the empty houses had been cleared, the whole area resembled the aftermath of a bomb raid, so for a bloke who had been brought up in The Blitz it was bliss. I rummaged through the dusty ex-homes finding rejected items that I could flog for a couple of bob. I found lots of old kitchen chairs and tables that were made of oak and I lost count of the WW2 tin hats that I found. None of the 'treasures' were worth much, but in bulk they made a difference to my pocket. Sometimes when I entered one of these ruins I felt that I was intruding, I could imagine the families who had lived there and silly old sod that I am I would feel sad, but I still took liberties with their leftover possessions.

When all the rest of the houses fell foul of the demolition crews I could stand in my garden and see all the way to Glyn Road and check up on who was entering our lively local pub, The George. The open space in between made us think that we lived in The Little House on the Prairie, this prairie was a magnet for the local kids, a ready made Adventure Playground.

When the 5th of November approached it was easy to pile up old timbers from the houses and make a huge bonfire. I did this all on my own because not many of our neighbours had my fondness for getting their hands dirty, so when I lit the fire there was only me and a straggly bunch of kids who had sensed that something was about to happen. As the flames started licking around the towering timbers something special happened. Lots of mums, dads and their kids swarmed out of their homes, some carrying fireworks and some bringing potatoes to bake. I was feeling very happy with the turn-out when it occurred to me that the lazy buggers had been looking out of their windows watching me knocking myself out and waiting for the easy bit of the Guy Fawkes celebration.

Then something happened that pleased me greatly and was to please me for years after. I heard someone call loudly "Oi Walker, is that the best you can do?" I turned round to see an old mate of many years, Georgie Mayo. Georgie stood there with a great big grin across his grubby face and looked as relieved to see me as I was to see him. "What are you doing here?" I said. "I've just moved in across the road " he replied, grinning even wider. This was music to my ears because I knew what a character he was, always happy, full of fun – and could talk and tell stories even better than me. " Come on, let's show'em what a proper bonfire is, get hold of those big timbers and we'll build up this excuse for a fire. Blimey, with a bit of luck we can have the Fire Brigade down here before too long, now that will be a good bit of fun!" So spurred on by George's couldn't-care-less attitude and his sense of naughtiness we acted like school kids and built the biggest, most dangerous fire that been seen since the war. Quite a few of the neighbours, who now seemed so ordinary next to George, stood back with worried looks on their faces and words of warning that George just laughed at. Rather disappointingly, the Fire Brigade never arrived.

BY GEORGE

Settle down now, make yourselves comfortable, because I am going to tell you about Georgie Mayo. I have just struggled to think of a descriptive word to put before his name but I had to admit defeat. I don't think there is such a word.

I'm not sure when I first met him. I do know we were very young and I do know that within a minute or two I liked him and his ability to make you an instant mate. He seemed to know half of the people in Hackney and it seems that they all liked him.

 I think they call it 'charm'.

He was one of those unique characters that made his own rules and definitely could not give a monkey's about conformity or 'image'. Fashion and trends just passed him by, he was happy to just be George.

He was short and stocky with a shock of almost curly, almost auburn hair that had a mind of its own and was prone to tumble down onto his forehead. He was seldom dressed smart but wore comfortable clothes that never looked new. He constantly had a smile on his outdoor complexioned face and a roguish twinkle in his eye, that's probably because he really was a lovable rogue. As the years went by he didn't alter much except that he lost a tooth here and there, but George being George he never let it bother him, and George being George it only added to his characterful boat race.

He had never quite come to terms with reading and writing and as a result he often mispronounced complex words, but he made sure that people knew what he wanted especially when it came to dealing. (I never said that he couldn't count.)

The most ordinary incident became an interesting or comical story when George got hold of it, he was a naturally skilled story teller who would by instinct set up a tale, describe the surroundings or the weather and the people involved, then bring it all to an end with a suitable punchline and a big grin. Give him a public bar and a group of drinkers and off he would go spinning his yarns. He dragged listeners in by making them think that he was only talking to them, he simply leaned forward putting his face near the listener's as if sharing a secret.

The Mayo family, and there were many of them, lived near Ridley Road Market where George and his mum and dad had a vegetable stall or, as George described it, selling "Tater and green, carrot and onion". Right up until the 1990s, their means of transport was a horse and cart, the horse being stabled in the back yard. I believe that George and his faithful nag Bill operated the last working horse-drawn cart in Hackney, possibly in London.

The pleasing pair would turn people's heads as they trotted along Kingsland Road on their way to the Old Spitalfields Market. They featured in a few newspapers and magazines and were always happy to pose for photographers.

One wet and windy morning George had his head down shielding his face from the bitter weather and Bill was hurriedly trotting home to his warm stable when a policeman, waving his arms wildly pulled George over. Our George was not pleased, but kept calm. "Do you know that you drove through a red traffic light?" said the over-keen copper. "I never drove through nuffink" replied George in an agitated way. "But I saw you" insisted Plod. The twinkle returned to George's eye as he said "It wasn't me, it was the bleedin' horse". I'm afraid that the weather had got to P.C. Happy, he was in no mood for nonsense and told George that he would report him to the Superintendant. George shrugged and scooted home.

A couple of weeks later an invitation to attend Old Street Magistrate's Court and to explain his bad behaviour to the beak flopped through the letterbox. George attended, forsaking the bus and taking his workmate Bill and, of course, the cart. Bill was parked outside the courtroom and George was called into the box to answer the charges. He stood in the dock with his well worn working clothes contrasting with the immaculate attire of the courtroom officials and filling the whole place with the smell of horses.

The magistrate told him that he was charged with jumping the lights and having faulty brakes on the cart. The copper got up and gave his evidence with relish, and now it was our Georgie's turn to address the court. With a hint of another twinkle in his mince pie he repeated the reply that he gave to the policeman "I never went through any lights, it was the horse". the Magistrate appreciated George's tongue-in-cheek statement and asked him to explain. "Do you know anyfing about horses?" he asked the copper. "If you did, you would know that the horse is in charge of the cart, he says what happens. He wanted to get home, that's what made him hurry". The Magistrate was now smiling, trying his best not to laugh. "And another fing" said George, now feeling his feet, "there ain't no brakes on a cart, again it is the horse's job to stop the cart", and cockily added "Don't you know nuffink?"

All of the occupants of the courtroom were now smiling along with George as he tried to explain that the thing that resembled a brake was just to stop the empty cart from running away. He then faced the beak and said "The horse and cart are outside, do you want to see it?" Believe it or not, the Magistrate, the lawyers, the copper and a lot of the public gallery descended the marble stairs and went outside to meet the very patient Bill, who was busy munching the bran in his nosebag. The combined charm of both George and Bill was too much for the band of admirers and they all patted and spoke to Bill. The magistrate called them all back to court, stood George in the dock and very happily pronounced "Case Dismissed".

When Hackney Council decided to 'enhance' the area around Ridley Road they compulsory purchased the Mayo house and stable yard. George was heart-broken and reluctantly let Bill and another horse go to another owner. The business needed transport so he bought a pick-up truck, he admitted that it was a lot more convenient and cleaner. He drove the truck for years without the need to be inconvenienced by such things as driving licences and tests. I think that the police did not fancy taking him to court again.

The Mayos had kept horses and dogs for many years before the area became intolerant of unique characters. As well as working, the horses took part in all the family events including weddings and funerals. When George's dad Tom Mayo died, a market funeral was organised, the cortege was to pass through Ridley Market. All the many Mayos gathered at the family home along with many friends, associates and neighbours. The B.B.C. sent a film crew and the very well known cockney presenter Monty Modlyn to make a record of this historic last bit of rustic East London. The procession was very moving, a dozen funeral cars followed the hearse and behind them followed many vans, pick-ups and lorries belonging to traders and admirers of Tom Mayo. But the most tear-jerking sight was at the front of the cortege. Bill the faithful horse led the procession draped in a mourning purple silk blanket, the wonderful Bill hung his head in deep sorrow all the way through the market bringing tears to many eyes. When the coffin reached the Mayo stall it stopped for Tom to take a 'last look' at his precious place in this famous market. The stall was draped in a pure white sheet and in the centre stood a highly polished set of brass weighing scales. The market fell silent, all the usual hustle and bustle and amplified music stopped, most of the stall holders stood by their stalls in tribute and Bill's head dipped even lower. When Bill led the procession again the silence continued. George was heartbroken.

Bill and George could be seen every year in the Horse and Harness Parade in Regent's Park and local carnivals but perhaps the most joyous event was when George's daughter, Sherry, got married. George had bought a tub-cart, that's a small trap, as in pony and trap. George worked on the cart varnishing, repairing and re-upholstering the seats so I knew he had plans for this delightful little vehicle. I should have guessed it was for the wedding. Sherry was getting married in Hackney Town Hall and the plan was for her to arrive in the tub-cart. Sherry had a beautiful white wedding dress and head dress, she did not want to reach the Town Hall looking bedraggled so I drove her to St. John's Church where a very smart George waited with his very proud Bill. I swear that this special horse knew what an important occasion it was, because now his head was held high with pride, I ushered the lovely bride into the wedding cart and our George beamed with pride and happiness, for once he had nothing to say. Then a clicking of his tongue and a gentle gee-up gave Bill the signal that he needed. With his head held higher than usual, he stepped out into Mare Street and trotted down the Narrow Way, his legs raised high between each step. Sherry glowed with radiance as the breeze blew her head dress trailing behind her and George, still silent, looked close to tears of pride. In the Narrow Way shoppers waved and shouted good wishes and a shop that Sherry worked in sent all the shop workers out to cheer her on.

    I followed on until we reached the town hall and the bride and her dad dismounted from the magical tub-cart. The guests followed them up the impressive steps to the front door and they all disappeared inside. During this special time I had a very important task, I stayed outside looking after dear old Bill!

UP BEFORE THE BEAK AGAIN

One day George went into one of the bigger DIY stores for materials for a job that he was doing. He drove the pick-up into the large car park and ambled across to the entrance, he was dressed in his usual 'very comfortable' working clothes. His disregard for high fashion must have alerted the security officer.

George walked up and down the aisles picking up all the materials that he needed, filling his arms and hands until it became a bit awkward to handle, so he stopped and rearranged his load. He put some items under his arm and put a small door catch in his pocket, he went to the till chatting to every-one as usual, especially the cashier, he paid for the articles and took the receipt. He then walked back to his motor, put his hand into his pocket to find the key and discovered the unpaid for door catch. Cursing himself, he dropped the materials into the cab of the truck and strolled back to the till to pay for the fiddly little door fitting. As he entered the lobby up came the security officer and accused him of shoplifting. Of course George explained the understandable cock-up but the officer was not in the mood for explanations and was certainly not understanding. He marched George to the security office and locked him in while he went for the manager, the manager was as hard as the security man and called the old Bill in. George's natural friendly nature flew out of the window.

In the Magistrates court the hard-hearted security man told a story of George acting suspiciously and 'lurking about'. He said that George had deliberately hidden the offending door catch 'on his whereabouts' and fled the store.

By now George had really got the needle and glared at the lying officer as he questioned him "When you nicked me, what direction was I going in?" "You were going to your car". George replied "No I wasn't, I was coming back to pay for the catch". "No, you were leaving the store" old nasty said. "What did I have in my hand when you pulled me in?" "Just the catch" was the reply. Then, with a hint of satisfaction, George produced the receipt, "Where were all these fings that I bought?" said George. "In your car" came the reply. "Well then, I must have been coming back" said our mate with his confidence coming back like a boomerang. "And another fing, do you think that I would stupid enough to nick anything when you were watching me all around the store. You never took your eyes off of me for a minute".

   The magistrate now asked the officer, "Is that right, did you watch him all the time?" "Yes" replied the now wary officer. "Why did you follow the accused?" asked the Magistrate, but before he had a chance to answer George shouted "Because he thought that I was a gypsy!" Mr. Magistrate looked at the security man and said "And did you think he was a gypsy?" "Yes I did" he said, as if he should be proud of it. The Magistrate took a deep breath and said "Case Dismissed!"

BROTHER BILLY

I have mentioned that there were hordes of Mayos. I have wracked my brain to remember all of them but have given up the job in frustration. However there was one of George's brothers who we got to know very well, the very likeable Billy Mayo, not of course to be confused with Bill the horse. Billy had a character of his own, he appeared to be shy but the truth is, unlike George, he never had too much to say,. There is an old Cockney saying that some people don't say much but think all the more, that sums Billy up.

He was softly spoken with a slight lisp and always a smile playing around his face, he was simply a nice bloke. His soft and slow manner led some people to think that he was just a bit simple-minded but they soon found out different if they took him for granted or tried to fiddle him.

Billy had a horse and cart too that he used for recycling waste products – that's right, he was a rag and bone man. A bit like Steptoe, he scoured the streets looking for scrap that could be turned into hard cash. This hard, dirty work never made too much money and was fraught with punters trying to get what they could from him, and that's where his soft, slow nature became a means of getting misjudged. One day he was drifting around the streets of Walthamstow mounted on the footboard of the cart (properly called a trolley) when an Indian man emerged from a house. "Do you want this old car engine?" he asked. Billy took a look at the dirty, oily engine that was nearly hidden by weeds that had grown around it. "Alright, I'll take it away for you" he offered. "Give me twenty five pounds for it" said this crafty Asian (I will let you put in your own answer to this impertinent demand). After a bit of bargaining, Billy agreed to give him a fiver for it."Give me a hand to lift it" he said, eyeing the messy, heavy eyesore that plagued the tiny front garden. "Not me" was the rude reply."I am not hurting myself and getting dirty doing your work" the cheeky bugger said. "You do it on your own".

In his usual slow manner Billy put his arms around the engine, and by some hidden strength struggled with it until it was on the trolley. After getting his breath back he took the horse by the reins and walked away down the road. After about one hundred yards old Crafty came running after him shouting "Give me my fiver!" Billy looked at him with disdain and gently said "There is a five pound lifting fee". "You can't do that" was that reply. " I've just done it" retorted the now pissed off Billy. "Give me back my engine" shouted the angry punter," I want it back!". Billy looked at him slowly and drawled "There it is, take it then".

Billy slid back onto the footboard and the horse clip-clopped down the street. They both left the chancer standing with one foot in the gutter and a disappointed look of defeat on his still clean face.

FANCY MEETING YOU HERE

Hackney Council continued their policy of 'improving' the area and in the process swept away the last half a dozen stables used by rag and bone dealers, including Billy Mayo's. Billy could not contemplate the thought of losing his horse and his traditional way of living, so he did what many locals felt they had to do, he moved out to pastures new. His particular pasture was in the Essex town of Basildon, a town that made it possible to carry on saving the planet by recycling Basildon's scrap.

At that time I was working as a lorry driver delivering frozen food, on this particular day I took a load to the newly opened Tesco at Pitsea. When I arrived at Tesco's yard I could see a queue of lorries waiting to be unloaded, so I decided to go for a cup of coffee and a bacon sandwich in the Cafe in the area of Pitsea Market. Outside the cafe stood the familiar sight of a totter's horse and cart, it made me think of Billy.

This cafe was one of those that was always busy. It served all the old fashioned Cafe fare, you know, everything fried and chips with it. On the counter stood one of those shiny silver steam machines that made the tea and coffee by sending clouds of hot steam into the cup and then to every corner of the room and making a loud noise that sounded like a jet plane was landing. The steam made the cafe 'foggy' and caused condensation to drip from the ceiling.

The place was packed and I had to sit at the only spare seat near the door. I gazed through the mist looking for a familiar face and it was then that I spotted our Billy. He was sitting at the other end of the long thin coffee shop grinning at me and giving me a wave. I did not want to lose my seat so called down the room "How are you Billy?" "I'm alright" he called back,."I thought that I recognised your horse" I said. We continued our high volume chat and by now the diners in the cafe were listening in and flicking their heads back and forth to who-ever was speaking. Then I called "Do you like it down here, Billy?" "Yes" he answered "it's smashing, all the people are so friendly ... except for that bloke across the road who owns that pub". "What makes you say that?" I said. "Well, this morning I took the horse and cart into his car park and he came running out shouting and calling me all sorts of names. Yeah, he said get that scruffy rubbish out of my pub and don't come back, you pikey" there was a pause and Billy said "But I got my own back on him, as we crossed the car park the horse done a fucking great big shit!"

Billy realised what he had said and burst out laughing along with all the rest of the customers.

FOR THE LOVE OF GEORGE

By 1977 we had been living on the estate for seven years and close friendships had blossomed between most of the families, people helped one another and stuck together when the need came. This was the year of the Silver Jubilee and it was decided to have a street party 'just for the kids' of course, a strong group of us planned the celebrations and in order to fund it we called at every door asking for weekly subscriptions.

This decision opened up one of the most hateful periods in our memories. Nearly all the tenants welcomed us at their doors and handed over the donations with excited expectations but one particular knock on a door started off a chain of events that carried on for many months. The family in this home were Irish and did not like the idea of anyone paying their respects to the Queen, told us in a most obnoxious way to "Eff off" and called us and Her Majesty English C***s. Now I am not any kind of Royalist but suddenly got upset that anyone should call 'our Queen' such a name, not to mention including us in this despicable description. The door was slammed in our faces and we cursed them, shrugged our shoulders and carried on.

The parents of this family were heavy drinkers but their two kids were nice and part of the local group of playmates, so we decided that both of them would be able to come to the party despite no subscriptions being forthcoming. This charitable act did not please the piss-heads, and so began a long period of drunken intimidation, threats and insults.

Almost every night they arrived home from the pub full of Guinness and vitriol and began a noisy tirade that made sleep impossible, making everyone wanting to choke the life out of them. With their legs buckling under the burden of such an enormous amount of alcohol they hung on to the parapet of the balcony and systematically worked their way along the flats insulting and threatening the tenants of each home. Nerves and tempers were stretched to the limits, but the depths of depravity were yet to be plumbed. A vicious atrocity committed by the I.R.A. that caused death, injury and destruction was lauded by this detestable pair, their late night celebration of the carnage was a step too far for a lot of us and yet again we went out to return the abuse and to tell them to shut up. Of course they told us what we could do with ourselves and then threatened us with a similar attack and a visit from a lorry load of 'Murphy's Men'.

Poor old George's flat was directly under their one so he had the added aggravation of them drunkenly bashing and crashing into the early hours of the morning. George and his wife Brenda were at their wits end. Neither of them were aggressive enough to do the obvious, but the obvious was dished out one very satisfying night.

On this particular night we could hear them coming down the hill, it seems that they could not wait to spread their particular form of evilness. A lot of the neighbours got out of bed to shout futile abuse at them, things were at fever pitch! They took up their position on the balcony and many of us gathered on our side of 'no man's land' ready to return the shit that they were shouting at us. Every time one of us cursed them they sent a threat back. You could feel the tension crackling in the air when they did something that really lit the blue touch paper. The gallons of booze that they had gulped down had the effect of making them puke the lot over the balcony. The Dirty Bastards!

Unfortunately George had left his window open and the contents of their alcoholic stomachs splashed into his window and on to his immaculate bed. The months of mental torture and humiliation sent George to the end of his tether and he came out screaming, raving and close to tears. The sight of our dear old George in such a state spurred on the usually placid neighbours.

Further along the block lived a bloke who was scared of no-one and had a long history 'taking care' of adversaries, I won't reveal his name, so let's call him Jim. Jim was a six foot three, tough Romany Gypsy and his loud gruff voice drowned out all the noisy schermozzle that was taking place. "Shut the fucking noise up" he shouted, "some of us want to get to sleep". The vile drunkard replied cockily "You can shut up, I'll come and get you tomorrow". What a mistake to make! Jim, who had just got out of bed and was stripped to the waist, calmly said "Don't wait 'til tomorrow, I'm coming over now". Jim crossed the great divide and some of us followed him, he mounted the stairs two at a time and at the top stood the source of all our despair and object of our hatred. He sparred up to Jim, and that was the second mistake he made that fateful night. Jim's club hammer-like fist landed right in the middle of his nasty face but he never went down, I think that Jim holding him up by the scruff of his neck may have had something to do with his ability to remain erect and to withstand the rest of the pasting that he richly deserved. Jim seemed so calm, and every blow was accompanied by a remark. The first gem was "Hold that!", then "Here's another one", "Did you like that one?", "Cop This" and so on. At that moment the Police arrived and first one up the stairs was a sergeant who valiantly stepped in-between Jim and his punch bag. Jim, being in full swing, caught the sergeant on the side of his face. "Oh, sorry Sarge!" said Jim still carrying on with the volley of punches. To my amusement and admiration Sarge said "That's alright mate". It seems that good manners ruled that night.

A very distraught George and Brenda came up the stairs and I tried to calm them down and see that they never did anything in front of the lawmen. My efforts were abandoned when a hateful scream came from the witch-like wife of the now groggy trouble maker. Brenda could not control herself after such a long period of torture and rushed at her with pent up anger and revenge in her mind. One of the onlookers told me to stop her, but I thought to myself "Give her a few minutes" and that is what I did. I have to admit that I got satisfaction by seeing Brenda sloshing the daylights out of the hated harpy.

A few fellow piss-heads who had drifted in from the pub attempted to come to the aid of their boozing pals but George's loyal friends saw them off with well deserved kicks up the arse!

Both of them started screaming again, this time their vitriol was directed at the Police. It was a pleasure to see them both handcuffed and finally shut up. The sergeant came to me and said "Where is your mate?" "What mate?" I said. "The big fellow who was stripped to the waist". "I've never seen him before" said I. The honourable Sarge had a look of resignation on his face as he said "I thought you might say that". I wanted to shake his hand, but thought better of it, however I did thank him.

George and Brenda stayed our close friends and neighbours for many years. George sadly died a few years ago followed by his beloved Brenda. Jim had a heart attack and died in a Betting Shop.

I believe the two evil bastards have died. Forgive me if I don't shed any tears over them!

THE WORST OF TIMES

So far in these tales I have tried to be light and humorous with 'salt of the earth', comical characters, but sometimes life can kick you in the teeth. I find it difficult to bring myself to tell you of a tragic episode that still makes me uncomfortable and extremely sad. So, with a lot of uncertain feelings I will try to do justice to this heart-wrenching tale.

After living on the estate for many years, we, without realising it, had become a strong community. In particular, a bunch of mates became close, mostly through our interest in cars. We got together on weekends and did all our repairs and servicing together, helping each other and going for a pint when all was done. There is no doubt that the strength of this 'car club 'centred around Elroy who was handy with a spanner and was always pleased to help any-one who needed his talents.

Elroy was a dapper little Jamaican bloke who always wore a knitted woollen hat pulled down to his eyebrows and sometimes even lower giving him the Rasta look. He was a typical Caribbean black man until he opened his mouth and a sharp Cockney accent flowed out. This bouncy, cheeky, charismatic star of a man always had a twinkle in his bright eyes and was known by everyone in Clapton, particularly in local pubs, shops and of course in car spares shops and garages.

He had a small car that he described as a 'proper black man's car', mainly because of his treatment of its looks. It had long, bendy aerials with the latest fad, fox tails, adorning them, wheel covers with spinners on them, fancy cushions on the back shelf and - most important of all - a record player that boomed out his music deafening everyone for streets around. He absolutely loved this motor and it showed!

He had a wife and three kids and lived above us. He was a perfect neighbour apart from his habit of playing very intrusive music that was amplified by some of the largest speakers that you have seen, made by his own very skilled hands of course. Whenever anyone challenged him about the noise he simply turned up the 'twinkle button' and charmed them, finishing off the pacifying with his winning smile. Nobody was immune to his smooth charm.

His wife and kids became dear friends of all of us and they seemed a perfect family. There were a few whispered rumours that none of us wanted to hear so they were ignored. I won't repeat these rumours because as far as I know that is all that they were.

It was clear however that something, whatever it was, was not right. Elroy was not as bouncy as usual and his willingness to help anyone was not there, what's more we suspected that he was drinking too much. He never appeared to be drunk but it dulled his natural charm.

One Saturday evening I was in the back of my van doing some little job or the other when Elroy appeared and climbed into the back with me. I asked him if all was well with him, he resentfully said that it was, but it was clear to me that he wanted to talk so I told him that I was here if he needed me and was ready to help him with any problems that he might have. A slight smile went across his face as he held my hand and said "Don't worry about me I can look after myself, any way I am going away soon and no-one around here will see me again." I said "What about me, will I see you?" He laughed and said "Oh yes, you will see me now and then". I knew that he had a bottle of spirit in his pocket so I told him to go home and sleep it off and that I would see him in the morning.

To be honest he was getting me down just a bit so I was pleased when he left me and headed in the direction of his house.

The following morning being Sunday the 'Car Club' drifted aimlessly together. "Where's Elroy?" someone asked. "Probably sleeping it off" I thoughtlessly said, so we carried on and finished up in the pub for a pint before dinner.

When I returned from work the following evening Elroy's wife was waiting for me. "Have you seen him?" she asked. "He hasn't been home for two nights, I'm a bit worried now". "When I have eaten I will look for him" I promised, so I popped into our nearby pub to ask if anyone had seen him. The answer was no so I wandered farther afield to a few of the other locals, but the answer was always no.

Now I was getting worried, and his seemingly empty threat of going away to where no-one will see him took on a new meaning. The following evening along with our mate Russell I revisited the pubs and clubs and even the shops, the answer in every place was a firm No!

Next day we looked in all the unusual nooks and crannies when the obvious struck us like a hammer blow. Elroy kept his precious car in a lock-up garage so we decided to break into the lock-up, just to be sure of course. Just as we neared the lock along came Ken, another member of the Car Club. "Hold on" he said, "I've got a key for this garage, Elroy lets me keep my tools in there." We opened the garage door with trepidation and a slight feeling of being over-dramatic, but these feelings were smashed when we saw his prize possession parked up. It was then that I feared the worst, he definitely would not go anywhere without this special motor.

I stared into the dark garage feeling sick and trembling like a leaf, and when I spotted a note behind the windscreen wiper my heart thumped in my chest. We looked inside the car and in the corners of the cramped garage but could see no sign of him, so I decided to look under the car. I crept on my hands and knees and stuck my head under the rear, it was pitch black and I could see nothing, but then my eyes became accustomed to the dark and gradually I could see a sight that I wished I would not see.

It was of course Elroy. As I had pushed my head into the darkness my face was just inches away from my dear mate and as he had been there for quite a few days it was a most terrifying experience.

    Common sense flew out of the window as I rushed to tell my wife. I was wearing a boiler suit and was attempting to take it off as I ran, causing me to stumble. We called the police and decided to go to tell Elroy's wife. Me and my wife climbed the stairs to perform this most unpleasant task. Elroy's wife was asleep in a chair. When Pam woke her and blurted out the appalling news she was not believed, but gradually the truth sank in. Of course the tears flowed from all of us. Later I had the even more heart-wrenching task of telling the kids that their Dad was dead. There were more tears.

    The next few days were a blur of high emotions, sorrow and guilt. Most people were shocked and deeply saddened by the loss of such a popular character and by the way in which he left us, but a few criticised him for 'breaking God's law'. Everyone had opinions and were willing to air them constantly. It was very wearing for us who knew him well but one person was to be a comfort to me. Me and Russell went into our local, The Glyn Arms, and sat down with a pint, the landlady, an Irish lady called Kathy, simply sat down with us, put her arm on mine and said "How are you Brian?" I poured out all the details of the very emotional past week and felt better for it.

    More heartbreak was to follow in that week when I accompanied Elroy's wife to the Coroner's Office to 'Identify the Body'. We stood in silence in front of a pair of curtains that covered a window, the curtains parted and there was Elroy. Well he looked like Elroy but all the twinkle, cheek and charm was absent. I remember thinking that the whole procedure was like a part of a Victorian Horror Show. I was relieved when the curtains were closed. It was then that the tears flowed again.

THE FUNERAL

There was resentment and tension between Elroy's and his wife's families, both blaming the other for the tragic outcome. These feelings spilled out at the burial. The funeral was, strangely, held at a church in Forest Gate, but this did not deter Elroy's many Hackney friends from cramming into the large building. If you have ever been to a West Indian funeral you will know that they are nearly always very busy affairs. Caribbean folk believe it is their duty to attend such ceremonies, admirers from local Irish pubs, workmates, and many of our local community joined the family to give him a good send off. He *did* have a memorable send off but not in any way that was planned.

The service was typical West Indian, plenty of tributes, prayers and hymns and of course lots of sobbing and sorrow. It was the interment that took on a life of it's own. It is the custom for mourners to use a shovel to throw a spade full of earth into the grave as a symbol of burial and after the graveside prayers the mourners stand around the open grave and sing hymns until they feel gratified. A prominent member of the church leads the singing and encourages the singers in a very 'gospel' way. I find it a very satisfying conclusion to such an emotional time.

As the first shovel of earth dropped onto the coffin the resentment and tension, which had been concealed, now burst forth with vigour and passion. The next shovel load was thrust into the hole only to be matched with even more vigour by a member of the opposing family who gave out a 'Praise to the Lord' followed by what can only be described as a burying contest, each frenzied thrust of the shovel being accompanied by a 'Hallelujah'. Now both teams of shovellers were ignoring the sequence and filling the once empty grave in just minutes. Two council grave diggers just stood by with

THE FUNERAL

blank looks on their faces. The gospel singing was treated with just as much vitality and competition. Some weeks later there was an inquest. I was the main witness, it all seemed so gentle and proper after the very eventful burial. A verdict of Suicide was reached, the coroner praised me for my clear and concise evidence and added that my help and support to Elroy's family was commendable. It was all very good but I was burdened with guilt, I thought that I should have realised what he meant when he said that he was 'going away to where no-one will see him again' and that I hurried him away just to finish some trivial job on the van.

SOME TIME LATER

After the funeral and the inquest Elroy's wife and kids were invited to stay with Elroy's brother who lived in the Midlands. Before they set off for a long visit I was asked to keep an eye on their place and was handed the keys, I popped in once a week to water the indoor plants and check that all was well.

One night I returned home late and glancing up I could see that all the lights were on. I thought that it was strange that no-one had phoned me to tell me of their return, nevertheless I went up to see them all. I knocked on the door but no reply. After a few more knocks I took the keys out of my pocket, opened the door and attempted to enter. What stopped me in my tracks was a peculiar smell and a film of smoke that filled the whole flat. The recent shock that I had suffered came immediately to my mind and I feared the worst. I am not ashamed to say that I was dead scared of what I might find if I entered. I dashed downstairs to my wife and our next door neighbour Rene, and shakily told them of my fears. Rene said "Don't be daft, I will come up with you, it's got to be done".

Rene's bravado disappeared as soon as I opened the door to the creepy atmosphere that lay inside, she pushed me to go in but I stood firm and tried to push her in, she was even more reluctant to make the first move than I was. Then, the eerie smell and smoke gripped us and there we both stood holding on to one another with our skin creeping. "Phone the police" she suggested and that is what we did.

Two coppers arrived in a very short time. I explained about Elroy and how we were simply too scared to go in. I had a feeling that we had planted the seed of fear into the policemen because they never said much as they cautiously crossed the threshold. We stood outside not saying a word for what seemed ages, so I called in "Are you two alright in there?" They never replied, but after two of the longest minutes that I have ever known they reappeared. "There is nothing to be afraid of but there has been a visitor" one said.

We were now brave enough to go in, when we did we found some very strange goings-on. All the chairs had been turned upside down, the bed had been stripped and an open bible placed on it and burning incense had been placed in the kitchen and bathroom. This accounted for the smell and the smoke. Then I worked out what it was all about. Elroy's wife's mother was an old fashioned West Indian Christian and it seems that she too had a key to the flat and had performed a kind of exorcist service to keep out the unwanted spirit of Elroy.

The chairs had been inverted so that he would not be comfortable and the bed had been made unwelcoming and protected by the bible. I'm sure that the incense had been lit just to scare the life out of me and Rene, if so it was successful!

All this was many years ago. Most of it has been forgotten by all but those closely involved in the tragedy, but a few months ago while visiting the Homerton Hospital we met Elroy's wife. There were hugs and kisses and questions about our health and wishes of good luck but not a mention of this story. Although we were all reminded of it, not a word was spoken.

MOVING ON

The traumatic and harrowing experience of Elroy's death had a profound effect on me, I never realised it at the time but looking back now see that it had altered my outlook on life. At that time I was working as a salesman for a national snack-food company. My ability to talk to people had made me very popular with my many customers and in the more than twelve years that I had spent at this work I had been very successful, resulting in me winning many incentive prizes and accolades. What is more I really believed in this job, I considered that we were 'helping to feed the nation' and that the work was so necessary. But now it seemed so trivial and powered by greed for money and possessions, I had simply lost faith in the whole thing. I was warned a couple of times about my attitude and when I found out from my loyal customers that a security man had been trailing me and asking questions about me I went to see the Regional Manager for a showdown. I told him of my recent tragic experiences and the effect that they were having on me, but the stone-hearted, money-conscious bugger just looked down at me and gave me a 'pull yourself together' lecture.

To my great satisfaction I told him exactly where he could shove his job and simply walked out on the spot. Standing outside of the depot I felt like a weight had been removed from my shoulders and that I was as free as a bird. This euphoria lasted for just a short time when I suddenly realised that I was out of work for the first time in my life. Within hours I met a neighbour and told him of my lack of a job. "You have got a Heavy Goods Driving Licence haven't you?" "Yes" I replied. "Call in to me tomorrow". So I went to another national food company and got a job as a delivery driver, all within hours of my stroppy walk-out. I spent three happy years with this friendly company who always looked after their workers.

MOVING FURTHER ON

This new job, although physically demanding, was so simple. No complicated paperwork, no stock taking, no pressure and certainly no-one spying on me. This freed my brain up to think of more creative things, since being a little boy I had artistic leanings (No Missus, not what you are thinking). Like most kids I liked drawing and painting and good stories and from my teens had taken up photography so you could say that I had an artistic bent (No Missus).

I had recently visited our old library that was now re-opened with the catchy name of Chats Palace. Here there were so many would-be and accredited painters, poets, actors and musicians all in one place, I just kept my eyes open and watched with wonder at these creative types. Cocky young sod that I was I thought that I could do that if I tried - so I tried! It wasn't as easy as I thought but with the encouragement of some of the local legends, namely Alan Rossitter and Freeform Arts, I persisted.

After about three years of working alongside such talent I gained enough confidence to go it alone and become self employed, but not having thought too much about exactly what I was going to do I found myself one bleak Monday morning scratching my head. I had dabbled in many things, such as performing, painting, making and organising events, but it was signwriting that felt most confident in and I knew that with my gift of the gab I could sell most things.

I walked out of my front door, crossed the road and saw that the Water Company had dug up a long section of the road in front of the local supermarket - obscuring the windows and giving the appearance that the store was not open. It took me just ten minutes to convince Mr. Singh that a large 'Still Open' sign would solve his problem of falling takings. So that was the answer, go out on the knocker to get work, and seeing as I was the boss and the entire work force of my new company I could still do my performing and other jobs that came my way.

TALES OF THE OLD PAINT POT

Of course I wasn't new to the art of lettering and soon settled into a routine of acquiring jobs and carrying out the work. I could tell you of the many and varied hand-painted signs that I did but that would literally be like watching paint dry, so I'll tell you a few tales associated with my dealings with customers and the public.

At first I found that working on my own was not as much fun as being with a crowd of workmates, but the good old 'man in the street' kept me company and amused, sometimes with friendliness and sometimes not. Because I mostly worked on the street I always was the centre of interest and attraction, I was almost a street entertainer, there was never a day that someone or two didn't stop to admire my work and to tell me that their granddad was a signwriter and that signwriting was a dying art, to which I always replied "Dying? I thought that I didn't feel well". Kids would come and watch and either tell me that I was 'brilliant' or more often that I was rubbish and once a big red faced Irish bloke looked at the very precise work that I had done and sniffed and declared that he had a twelve year old daughter who was much better than me. One day I was painting a large window in Kensington when out of the corner of my eye I could see someone watching me, I turned my head and came face to face with Bob Geldof. All these encounters gave me yet another story to tell and when I arrived home each night my wife asked me "Anything happened today?" then I would tell her in details of the dealings that I had with my admiring or sometimes not so admiring public.

Once I had a big job signwriting and illustrating a large supermarket in Well Street, Hackney. I took over a week to finish it and in that week I made a couple of unusual friendships. The very busy staff in the supermarket had no time to deal with me as I worked on the pavement outside in this little market, but opposite was a dental surgery and the two delightful young receptionists walked across the road twice a day with coffee for me and to see if I was alright, just good old fashioned manners and consideration that made me admire them.

On my first day there I had the inevitable 'ponces' who tapped me for money, "Just a pound or two" was the normal request, and after the third 'earnest appeal' I finally told them in a loud voice to Go Away, but in my own inimitable way of course. Just after my very public instructions to let me get on with my work I was approached again, this time by a young woman who pathetically asked for "a pound please". I felt the F-word forming in my mouth but something about her made me dip my hand into my pocket and resist giving her a mouthful of abuse. She was about 25 and would have been attractive if the ravages of her very obvious drug habit had not stripped her of any self-esteem. Her weathered face and her dull eyes were only matched by her dried up lips and stiff un-combed hair but she had a genuine pitiful look about her and somehow I felt sorry for her and handed over a couple of quid along with a well meaning lecture about taking care of herself and to pack up taking 'that shit'. I believe that she thought that for the first time she had found someone who cared enough to be interested in her welfare and thanked my profusely.

The next day she returned and I offered her some breakfast money, I could see that she was desperate to take it but some decency in her made her refuse it because I had already given her some, but I insisted that she take it and buy a cup of hot tea and a sandwich, which to my surprise she did. She returned to thank me and to show me her breakfast, I was flattered by her seeing me as some kind of person to impress by good behaviour.

On the third day she arrived looking a bit more human and

picked up a box and sat on it to watch me working. We chatted as I worked and she told me that she was from Sussex where she had lived with her mum and dad, she had ambitions to be a vet but all these plans were forgotten when her parents found out that she was a lesbian and disowned her. I, of course offered her comfort, advice and another cup of tea. She sat on that box all day keeping me company. When I got home from work I relayed this touching story to my wife who was immediately concerned for her welfare and gave me a pair of warm gloves and a scarf to keep her from getting cold and asked if she should make some sandwiches for me to take to her.

I worked for another few days and my new-found friend sat on her box alongside me for most of the time like some faithful guard dog. I felt quite sorry as I said goodbye to her when I left. I also walked across to the Dentist's shop to thank the lovely young ladies and they insisted on presenting me to the very gentlemanly dentist. I was honoured.

I passed the supermarket many times in the weeks that followed, each time admiring my handiwork and looking out for the pathetic young woman whose name I never even asked. But I never saw her again.

I had my faith in human kindness affirmed many times by caring Londoners. When I was working in Peckham in bitter cold conditions I was kept going by two lovely maternal Jamaican ladies who worried about me and constantly called me across the road to supply me with piping hot, deliciously spicy 'Cow Foot Soup' and to demand that I stand by the oven to thaw out. In Rotherhithe I was decorating a Burger Van on a bit of waste land when a barmaid from the local pub came trotting across the road with a tray complete with a pint of beer and a huge sandwich, "compliments of the Guv'nor" she said with a lovely smile on her equally lovely face, and in Tottenham a Turkish bloke insisted on me having half of the delicious packed lunch that his wife had supplied him with. These kind acts always moved me and I could rattle off many examples of decent people acting in such a considerate manner.

I had one regular customer, a Hungarian caterer, who gave me a lot of work. We both had a mutual trust of each other, he would phone me and tell me that there was a job in one of his catering units in a market or on one of his many catering trailers in his large yard. He had great confidence in my work and would leave me to design and compose the script for the jobs. I would carry out this work without money being spoken of, he never mentioned it neither did I, but he always called me to rave about the 'lovely' work that I had done for him. I asked him not to give me any money until I asked for it and once a year I would give him a bill for all that he owed me, well not so much a bill but a figure. He would without question tell me to go to the market where he simply handed me a paper bag full of bank notes. This honourable man trusted me implicitly and I trusted him, he was a real gent. I never let him down and he always came up trumps for me. This bag of readies would finance our annual holiday, where we drank a toast to him.

Now come the stories that you have been waiting for, tales of the many nasty, scheming, fiddling, thieving bastards who I was unfortunate enough to come face to face with.

I have had so many lies, excuses, tricks and downright refusals to pay laid on me that it is a wonder that I am still the same old kindly, trusting bloke that I always was, well perhaps not quite so trusting. The most common trick was to ask me for a price to 'put my name over the door', I would give a fair quote and a promise to return to carry out the little job but when I did return I would be handed a scrap of crumpled paper with what we signwriters call 'The Lord's Prayer' on it. A couple of days work for the price of a few letters. Leave it out mate. Many times when giving a quote I was told that it was too much and that the bloke down the road wanted to do it for twenty five quid, to which I always replied "Well let him do it" as I slammed the door on my way out. Another common blag was to pay me on completion of the job but not the full amount. "Come back on Friday for the remainder of the money" they often said, you've guessed it, Friday never came. I recall that one day my wife accused me of getting too cocky. "Cocky?" I asked, "If I don't get cocky I will be trampled on". There was a lot of truth in this observation. I had to curb my natural trusting nature and hone my 'butch, aggressive manner', yes I was getting cocky!

All signwriters use a 'stick', that is a length of dowel with a ball on the end, it's simply an aid to keeping your hand steady, but it is the first thing that onlookers notice and scratch their heads over. It's a crucial bit of our kit.

One day as I was working I heard a noisy trio of pimply faced yobbos coming in my direction, they were about 17 or 18, and full of something that made them mouthy, a bit threatening and giggling at every little thing. As they passed me the one with the biggest gob picked up my stick and waved it around his head causing the other two idiots laugh like silly kids. I stood up trying to look bigger than I really am and shouted "Oi you, give me that back!" No prizes for guessing that he told me to Fuck Off! He then proceeded to prance like a fairy down the road and waved the stick like a magic wand, well it did work some magic, it turned me into a my more unreasonable self. I followed the dopey trio and decided that there was nothing better than direct action, so I grabbed the stick and tried to yank it from his grasp but the sneering git held on even tighter.

Every time that I tugged it he tugged it back, now I was getting a real cob on and putting on my most aggressive face I snarled "GIVE IT BACK TO ME!" The sickly looking tripe-hound who was grinning so widely that he showed off a mouthful of rotten teeth, stuck his face near to mine and sneered "Make Me!" as he tugged it again. I could feel my mum pushing me in the back and saying "Don't forget what I told you" so I I didn't need to be told twice. I let go of the stick with one hand and used the other hand to deliver a hefty smack right round his dirty earhole. He stopped smiling as his head moved about 45 degrees out of true, but he still held on to the precious stick. Oh well, he asked for it I thought as my steel toecap made contact with his shin and at last he changed his mind about ownership of the now crucial stick. I held the stick across my chest like some war trophy as he limped down the road with one hand on his ear, his sidekicks stood with mouths open staring at me, so I took one step forward and growled at them, they overtook old Mouthy in their flight away from me.

Me, cocky? I was just getting the hang of this cocky business, what's more I was loving it!

I had the opportunity to show off my newly discovered cockiness again, this time with a bit more humour. When I was writing the name of a shop I was at the top of quite a long ladder and for reasons of security placed my kit directly underneath the ladder, all I had to do was to peer between my legs to keep an eye on my precious brushes and paintpots.

I was concentrating on the job when I caught a glimpse of a movement below me, it was someone lifting my box and creeping off with it. I came down that ladder like I was in a Charlie Chaplin film and grabbed the rather weedy, ancient tea leaf. He was Irish and an obvious alcoholic "Give me that back" I said as I snatched the box. Instead of arguing or being put out by being caught he gave me a performance that should have been nominated for an Oscar. In a quaking feeble voice he said "I'm starving, I've not eaten today, I feel so ill, give me a couple of quid". I knew that any money given to him would be pissed up the wall, so I told him that I would take him to a nearby cafe and buy him a cup of tea and a bacon roll. Suddenly a miracle occurred, his feeble voice got better and he called me all sorts of names at full volume, of course this was the perfect time to enhance my cockiness skills so told him in an even louder voice than his to "Go away! I'm not giving you money to buy booze" and for good measure I repeated my instruction to do something with himself. At that stage in stepped an African accomplice who shouted for all to hear that I was "A Racist!" "How do you work that out?" I asked, "You are only refusing to give him money because he is Irish, was the pathetic reply. "Oh yeah" I said "but I am Irish" I said lying through my teeth. "Yeah? What is your name then?" said the little man from the Emerald Isle. I stood up and faced the scrawny pair and said "Riley, now piss off!"

I'm afraid that I had left my cockiness at home when approached by a man who said that he had been told that I was the best artist in East London and that my theatrical set building skills were second to none. Well the truth was that I had some experience at these skills and that my efforts had been reasonably successful, but my ego had been massaged and I got carried along with his over the top appraisal. He had acquired a restaurant on the canal side in Bethnal Green and wanted to attract lots of theatrical diners, so he decided to produce a Musical Show. He had hired writers, composers, actors, musicians, dancers and me to create this threat to the West End.

I designed and built an intricate and complicated very large set, all the time being assured that I would be paid as soon as the production was staged. Well the production was staged, we were invited to the opening night where we mingled with a few film stars and TV personalities, to tell the truth the meal was pretty good, the show was very enjoyable and I was told many times what a talented designer I was, so far so good, but this opening night show was the only one that ever graced this stage.

It seems that this East End entrepreneur was something of a Walter Mitty so I and all the rest of the company never saw a penny in spite of my constant efforts to practice my macho cockiness on him. He was I'm afraid to say, just a bit cockier than me.

He owed me over a grand so I was not at all pleased, but about a fortnight later I went past the now closed restaurant and the door was ajar so I barged in as bold as brass to see a few men dismantling the interior of the once plush eating place. In the corner stood a nice little piano, it wasn't the brand new one that had only been played once but it was decent enough, so, using my acting skills I called out to the workmen "I've come to take the piano away" "It's over there" they said "Oh good, can you give me a hand to put it into the van?" They obliged me and I drove away and sold the Joanna for £150.

I heard that Walter Mitty finished up in jail.

I once carried out a nice big job on a Burger Bar in East Ham, the owner, a large friendly Turkish bloke had all the traditional Turkish traits of hospitality, he wasn't happy until he had filled your belly whenever you visited his restaurant. His name was Hassan and it was impossible not to like him, he constantly told me of how good my work was so I liked him even more. I made a huge shop sign that went above the premises and was a source of pride for me, he beamed with joy. Then I made a large intricate menu board that almost ran the length of the shop and I decorated the edges with tomatoes, onions, garlic and so on, "Put some horseshoes for good luck" he asked, so I felt like a kid with a new box of paints as I fitted horseshoes, flowers and other symbols in between the burgers and kebabs, I never wanted to stop. Hassan hugged me and dabbed at his very moist eyes as he told me that I was 'the best artist in the world' as he piled food onto my compulsory lunch. He paid me with great pleasure!

A couple of years later I got a call from the genial Hassan, telling me that he now had another restaurant and that I just had to do my wonderful work on it. "I want it the same as the other one" he said as again he told me that I was the best artist in world. So I did it!

When it was finished he again got emotional, said it was

marvellous, kissed me on both cheeks and said come back on Friday and I will pay you. Friday came and I returned full of myself, but this euphoria crumbled when Hassan said "I've got no money to pay you, any way I don't like it, It's Shit!" My heart sank! The amiable Hassan had disappeared and an aggressive, snarling oaf had taken his place, of course we had some very loud words and I went home with an empty pocket and not even the promise of an artery blocking tuck-in.

    I went back every night with a face like thunder but nothing came my way, one night a week later I found him playing cards with a very ropey looking mob. "Oh" he said "I had your money for you but now I have gambled it away." Talk about rubbing your nose in it! I decided that a change of strategy was called for. So… the following week, after biding my time I made a surprise call at half past one in the morning. I parked the van right in front of the door and made a bold entrance. Trading had finished and the staff were cleaning up and … counting the takings! I asked for Hassan only to be told that he wasn't there. As I stood fuming away I saw that one of the staff had taken the drawer out of the automatic till and was loading bags of coins into it. I had the sense to wait until it was full and cockily, (there's that word again) picked up the drawer and calmly walked out of the door and threw the contents onto the floor of the van.

    Then my decent upbringing overcame my common sense, fool that I am, I respectfully returned the drawer to the till giving the 'absent' Hassan time to miraculously reappear from wherever he was. He was not at all pleased, I could tell by the way he was waving a large, sharp kebab knife at me. My army training never mentioned anything about repelling kebab knife attacks, but I stood my ground with the drawer across my chest for protection.Hassan stared at me, I think he was more scared than I was, and a stand-off took place. Well, someone had to make a move and it was me, screaming some Celtic war cry I hurled the drawer at him and scooted as fast as I could into my van where I broke the speed limit on my way home.

Back in the safety of my home, me and my wife counted out all the one pound coins. For your information there was only £260 out of the £600 that he owed me, but at least I still had all my fingers!

When I tell people that I worked as a signwriter they often say "Oh that was a nice easy job!" Not on your Nelly, Missus, what with hanging from the top of a ladder for hours or scrambling up scaffolding, standing all day in the freezing cold or baking sunshine it was no picnic but I never ever got over my childhood joy of drawing and painting, what's more I got paid for it. (Sometimes.)

THE ROAD TO HOLLYWOOD

During all the many years that I spent, selling snacks, driving lorries, sign making and organising events, my head was full of daydreams, I thought that one day someone, somewhere would spot me and whisk me off to Hollywood. I had these dreams from being a teenager but being a realist knew that they were just a fantasy, but that did not stop me from getting involved in painting, photography and more dreaming, just for the fun of it of course.

I was involved with all my neighbours in organising the Silver Jubilee Street Party, and to that end we gathered unwanted goods and had a jumble sale. The small mountain of grotty jumble was taken to Chats Palace, then fairly unknown, and flogged off giving the party fund a nice boost. While we were knocking out toot I was approached by a bloke who told me of the grand plans that he had for Chats, as we called it. He wanted to turn it into a Palace, a community centre for everyone in the area, I looked around the once pristine Library that was now reduced to a shambolic building site and thought "No Chance Mate". As I was busy taking money for old rope he was hindering me so I gave him the cold shoulder, but he wouldn't be beaten by my rudeness and returned to pile his dreams next to mine. What a pain in the arse I thought, but something in his determination and imagination grabbed me, I had never met anyone like him before, a fantasist who genuinely believed in his dreams, and somehow got me thinking about them too. That was the first time that I met Alan Rossiter, the one who was to encourage me and make me realise just some of my own fantasies. "There's a Party on tonight" he said "come along, there's a good band on". I went and was captured, hook line and sinker.

Those early days at Chats Palace were both exciting and puzzling, I never knew exactly what was going on or who was who, but I was able enough to tell the many daydreamers from the more down to earth, practical people who had plans for the future.

Within a few weeks along with some of my family and friends I became a regular visitor and deeply involved in things that I had never even considered before. For instance I helped out with the Pantomime, that's right, me mucking about with kid's stuff, who would have thought it? I was soon to learn that it was not kid's stuff nor it was not mucking about. I helped with slapping a bit of paint about, a bit of woodwork, running errands and making the tea, but just do not ask me to perform, no, not at all.

Well, you guessed it, just like the stories in many corny musical films, on the opening night one of the walk on parts declined to appear so at the last minute someone said "Brian, you can do that".

Full of my own importance and carried along with the first night excitement I said "Of course I will", then sat down to realise that I had let my mouth get me into a situation that I didn't want. The Panto started and my two minute appearance became nearer and nearer. "Why did I say yes?" I muttered to myself as my legs became weak with fear and my stomach turned over for the tenth time. All I had to do was to walk onto the stage, attempt to sing a song and get eaten by a giant man-eating plant, but I had never sung in public before let alone acted, and what if the plant drops me?

All these fears hung heavy on my shoulders as I shakily climbed the step and entered the Magic Garden. The theatre lights blinded me, the audience seemed to be staring at me just waiting for me to do something wrong, everything seemed silent and so unreal and when I tried to sing nothing seemed to come out. I just hoped that someone would get me out of this bloody stupid panto, when my prayers were answered, the giant man-eating plant grabbed me, turned me upside down and swallowed me whole, phew it was all over! Then came the best part, the packed audience laughed out loud and gave us a big round of applause. It was marvellous and, fears or not, I could not wait for the next night's performance. Blimey, I was now an actor!

I went on to perform in nearly all of the pantomimes that were staged at Chats Palace.

In the very early days the late Mike Gray, local historian and one of the founders of Chats Palace, was instrumental in getting a Blue Plaque put up outside the Hackney house that Music Hall super-star Marie Lloyd had lived in. To celebrate he staged an Old Time Music Hall at Chats Palace. It was so popular that regular shows were put on. Mike asked me to come to see one, I tried unsuccessfully to avoid going to such a dated, old fashioned show, but just to keep him quiet I met Mike in the bar and reluctantly entered the auditorium.

It looked so dark and colourless, and when the performance opened with the chairman asking us to drink a toast to Queen Victoria I nearly got up and left. It was so prissy, and too theatrical, but those old songs were the songs that we had all been brought up on and sung in all the pubs and the beauty of them was that they did not have to be learned, they were there, in our heads. Next time a Music Hall was staged, I asked Mike if he wanted a hand to set up and in his very bohemian way he told me to do what I wanted to and disappeared leaving it to me, so with the help of John Scott and Inky Costin a new brush swept clean. We had no budget, so it was down to our scrounging and making do customs to inject a new look into what we considered to be a dry and dusty atmosphere. Somehow, I got my sticky fingers on to a roll of red lining cloth which we pinned up around the stage, got some candles which we stuck into beer bottles and went to the bomb dump opposite Chats to pick flowers that had bloomed there ever since the houses were destroyed in the war and put them in jam jars on the tables.

Over the next few months we poked our noses into every corner to scrounge whatever we could, Dickie Downes a well known local singer and pub landlord donated a large painted backcloth and I painted panels to adorn the walls. Me and John made ourselves pearly suits and greeted the punters at the door, ran the raffle and put the proceeds of this raffle into our materials fund, Eventually I became responsible for booking the artists and John and me were promoted to being "Plastic Pearlies", so began over 15 years of monthly shows in our own East End style.

This was the longest run of shows that Chats had staged.

The reputation of the Music Hall spread and eventually we were performing twice or sometimes three times a month, not exactly record-breaking, but for us it was thrilling. We were asked to go to clubs, homes and community centres now and then and, when a group of dignitaries from the Caribbean visited, Hackney Council put on a show and asked The Plastic Pearlies to take part. What's more they offered to pay us, what a thrill!

The show was staged in Stoke Newington Municipal Theatre and the audience flooded in packing the large hall to capacity. The welcoming speeches were made and groups of ethnic singers, dancers and poets wove their magical spells in front of the very appreciative audience. Then the compere announced : "The Plastic Pearlies!" and me and John stumbled awkwardly upon this huge and empty stage.

The silence was deafening as the multi-cultural audience stared at two very uncomfortable cockney blokes who for some unknown reason had sewed lots of buttons onto their suits and sang ridiculous songs like 'I've got a Lovely Bunch of Coconuts'. We left the stage to the sound of our own footsteps. At the reception after the show we were presented to the Mayor of a West Indian town who stared at us, screwed up his face and said "What are you supposed to be, are you clowns?" So much for 'Hands across the sea'!

In spite of this humiliation, I had my feet under Hackney Council's comfortable table and was asked from time to time to take part in and sometimes to compere events.

Then our dreams came true and out of the blue our beloved Hackney Empire re-opened after years of Bingo playing. I volunteered my services and was asked to produce a Traditional Variety Show to mark the re-opening and to raise funds for this beautiful theatre. I decided to present the show as a production of Chats Palace Music Hall, then unknown outside of the East End, but actors and variety stars begged me to be included in this historic event.

I was now getting very confident, or full of myself if you like, and managed somehow to get Anne Shelton, the legendary wartime singer to top the bill and with the help of many Chats Palace friends and members managed to pack the Hackney Empire to capacity. Of course, with all the many artistes fighting to get on the bill for this historic performance, we over-ran, but it had enhanced my reputation.

After this success I was offered many opportunities to produce events for councils, organisations and clubs, not least of all Hackney Arts and Entertainments, the local council. Variety shows, Tea Dances, Talent Contests and best of all, three seasons of Traditional Variety Shows at the Hackney Empire. At that time most of the old venues had closed but there were still lots of variety artistes about and, with a bit of asking about, it was easy to get them to come to Hackney and later to Chats Palace.

The next few years saw me working all over the place, from the South of France to Glasgow in venues that ranged from Grand Theatres to scruffy pubs, festivals, the backs of lorries, and even busking in Brick Lane Market. I couldn't resist any offer to get in front of an audience.

In Hackney, because of my many local appearances and the fact that our local newspaper The Hackney Gazette seemed to have my face in its pages at least once a month, I was getting known. I would occasionally be stopped in the street and recognised.

All the time this theatrical work was going on I kept my signwriting work going, working in the streets of our good old Hackney. One day I was working in Homerton High Street on a shop front and made a few drips of paint on the pavement, so I went down on my hands and knees with a rag and a bottle of white spirit, while I was rubbing away I was tapped on the shoulder by a lovely old couple. "Aren't you the bloke who does all the shows at the Empire?" they asked with a puzzled look on their faces. "Yes, that's me" I said in reply, "What are you doing that for?" I felt like a bit of fun and thought that I would make them laugh, so said "I'm doing community payback work, I threw away some paper in the street and have been sentenced to clean all the pavements in the area". I waited for the laughter to begin but not even a little titter left them. "Oh, that's not right, not after all the good work you do". I tried to explain that I was pulling their legs but they continued in their protest against the injustice that had been meted out to me. "Bloody council, fancy them picking on you, they ought to get these bloody pavements mended, not scrubbed by you, it's disgusting". They shambled on along the street still cursing the idiots who did not know what they were doing. I never had the nerve to tell them the truth.

Without even trying I got half a dozen very brief appearances on TV and when I was asked to act in a film I didn't so much think that I was on the road to Hollywood but I felt that I may be at the bus stop waiting for the coach to grind along to squeeze me into a back seat. Well, the bus never arrived and the glimpses of me on the box went by unnoticed by the mass media and the film was possibly the worst thing ever made. I did have a couple of responses to my couple of lines of dialogue, both saying "Was that really you in that awful film?" and giving me a look that unmistakeably said "Why?"

So it was back down to earth and reality.

MY HERO

During my time I have worked with a lot of well known performers and a few legends, and once I even had breakfast with Mr. Blobby, but I am not a name-dropper so will spare you the ordeal of Googling these names as you scratch your head and say "Who?" However there is one star, for that is what he was, who I am thrilled to tell you about. I was asked to produce a Variety show for The Greater London Council, this show was to be performed four times over one very heady weekend, on the South Bank no less, two performances in the very prestigious Queen Elizabeth Hall and two in the then County Hall. The tickets were avidly sought after due to the headliner. We hear the word legend bandied about these days but this was a true legend, some-one who spanned the generation gap and even today is very relevant, Ladies and Gentlemen, I present to you the much loved ... Clive Dunn.

Generations of TV addicts admired Clive for his many appearances in series such as Bootsie and Snudge, Grand Dad and of course his portrayal as Corporal Jones in Dad's Army. He started his career just after the war and stayed busy until just a few years ago, and of course Corporal Jones still lives on.

Back on the South Bank, when the compere announced him there was an air of expectation that was lived up to, the band struck up his play-on music and suddenly there he was, the one and only Corporal Jones complete with battledress and a battered bugle. The audience went wild and he hadn't spoken a word, such was the affection for both Clive and the immortal Corporal Jones. He told stories, cracked jokes and did a song and dance routine but, when he was joined by two young Hackney girls and they sang his big hit Granddad, you could feel the love and warmth throughout the theatre, such a corny, sentimental but moving song swept everyone into blissful nostalgia.

After the show we all sat in the bar overlooking the Thames and chatted and sipped drinks with this lovely humble man. It was a perfect ending to a perfect day.

I did a couple of more shows with him and told him about Chats Palace. He was fascinated and almost demanded that I ask him to perform there, so that is what we did. He was such a down to earth, kindly, genuine bloke, a life-long socialist and now a fan of Chats Palace. He absolutely loved the place and sat talking into the early hours until we chucked him out. We struck up a friendship and he sometimes would phone me for a chat, whenever he did I would smile because he sounded just like Corporal Jones, well, he would, wouldn't he?

Now in the year of 2016 Clive and Corporal Jones are very much back in the public's eye due to the making of the new Dad's Army film, not that they ever went away.

Clive, I remember you with affection, Corporal Jones I salute you! I'm sorry readers but I just have to say it …"Don't Panic!"

YOU LUCKY PEOPLE

Soon after the South Bank triumph I was asked to produce a season of Variety Shows at Stoke Newington Assembly Hall and of course turned to my new found friend Clive. He was pleased to be asked and with the aid of a group of pupils from William Patten School we packed the theatre out. All very good but I had now set the bar very high so I needed to find another headliner with the fame and credibility of Clive Dunn for the next show in the series. After scouting around I was offered the chance to book that star of stage, screen and radio, the one and only Tommy Trinder. Tommy was a legend who had topped the bill for many years, he had appeared in West End theatre, in films, on radio and television. It was he who was asked to compere the very first series of the very famous, long-running, record-breaking 'Sunday Night at the London Palladium' long before the immortal Bruce Forsyth was heard of, so it was a feather in my cap to make such a prestigious booking.

Tommy was by now quite old and had recently survived a massive heart attack. But every cloud has a silver lining, and this terrible attack had catapulted him back to the headlines.

I was a bit over-awed when I phoned him, after all there was me, a chancer from Hackney, addressing the great Tommy Trinder. Well I need not have been nervous because when he answered the phone and I respectfully said "Hello Mr. Trinder", "Call me Tommy, son" came the reply in that familiar, confident London voice.

We chatted briefly and I told him about the show. "It's in Stoke Newington" I said. "Stoke Newington? I went out with a girl fom there. Yes, that's right, Dynevor Road". "We are working for Hackney Council" I added. "My brother works for a council, Brent!" said he. Then he continued, "A couple of weeks ago I went into a theatre that I last went into in 1939, when I was there I scratched my initials into the paintwork of the dressing room, do you know, those bloody initials were still there. The place had never been decorated in all those years"

He went on to chat about things that were just as mundane and as I took my leave of him he very thoughtfully thanked me for the call and the job. I liked him very much.

A week before the date I called him again, this time saying "Hello Tommy". "Hello son" he said "How are you?" I reminded him of our date and he said that he was looking forward to it, then added "That's the one in Stoke Newington". "Yes" I replied. "I went out with a girl from there, Dynevor Road", and he went on to repeat word for word the conversation that we had already been through in our previous call.

I made allowances for his age, and perhaps his memory, simply because I was talking to one of Britain's most successful performers, and don't forget that he was such a nice old man.

Come the day of the event, and we were all fussing about preparing and rehearsing on the large stage when in came a rather insignificant figure. I approached him and immediately saw that it was Tommy Trinder. There was no mistaking that cheeky grin that sat above his trademark projecting chin.

I shook him by the hand and introduced myself. Of course he had never seen my before so he stared at my mighty beard and said "Blimey, if I have another heart attack I don't want you to give me mouth to mouth resuscitation." We laughed and he then said "I used to go out with a girl from here, Dynevor Road" then continued to re-repeat word for perfect word the same conversation that we were now hearing for the third time.

I tried my best to hide my boredom as I stifled a yawn and took him to his dressing room.

The show started and progressed to the Top of the Bill spot. Jim McManus, our compere, thrillingly introduced this latter day Super Star. We all stood by to admire the variety act of a legend. Jim gave him a marvellous build up and there he was, the incomparable Tommy Trinder.

The audience of 500 or so applauded, cheered and whistled at the sight of him causing a smile to spread across his very familiar face. As the intro music subsided he went to the front of the stage, looked at his admirers and said "Good Evening, You Lucky People."

The whole of the audience and most of the cast replied with gusto and gave him yet more noisy applause. He looked every inch a master of his trade as he stated "It's nice to be here in Stoke Newington." Another round of applause. "I used to go out with a girl from here" - yet more applause. "Dynevor Road" - this time they were nearly hysterical as they applauded with even more enthusiasm.

"My brother works for the council"- this time a cheer! "Brent!" Brent council was at that time the centre of all the loony left jokes and the one word simply had them all in howls of laughter.

Then we had the tale of the unpainted dressing room and other such trivia, but trivia or not every word was lapped up and reacted to.

If we were waiting to see a polished, well thought out act then we were disappointed, but we did have a lesson in stage presence and star quality.

When Tommy sang a song that was written for him his adoring audience were thrilled. The song? "Maybe it's because I'm a Londoner!"

A couple of years later I was involved with in the making of a film about Max Miller. In this film were many variety stars including Tommy Trinder. I never saw him during the filming but when we all attended the premiere at the Theatre Museum in Covent Garden he arrived. He was now of course two years older and time had taken its toll. He was now in a wheel chair and had lost a bit of weight. He looked all of his years, but in spite of his fragile appearance he was still the cheeky, jocular, noisy Tommy Trinder complete with that special grin.

I went up to him to reminisce, but he never remembered me. I was disappointed of course.

THE LONG AND THE SHORT OF IT!

Chats Palace drew in many people, some good, some bad, some interesting, some bloody boring and some who somehow stay in your mind and your affection. One such person was Dave Dutton.

My Dad, when he was in his late 70s worked a couple of days a week using his many building skills to maintain and decorate the building, Dave was then given the job of cleaning and generally taking care of maintenance so naturally the pair of them came into daily contact.

What a pair they made, there was Dad, a dapper, short-arsed cockney and there was Dave, a tall, gangly, slow talking country lad, what is more Dave was a Punk! My old man, always neat and tidy, shoes polished, trousers pressed, contrasted with the very scruffy, awkward looking Dave. Dave's legendary worn out look earned him the nickname of Dirty Dave, a name that he was quite proud of.

The punk style of that time demanded an alternative look and Dave embraced the demand with gusto, his hair looked like he had upset the barber, long in places, shaved in some other places and never ever groomed.He often wore at least two shirts - neither of which had seen a flat iron in their lives - and his stained and grimy jeans looked like his knees had exploded blowing ragged holes in them. His heavy boots, scuffed and worn so much that the steel toecaps peeped at you through the stained leather, were either too big or too heavy causing Dave to lumber around the building like Frankenstein's monster.

This duo, very different in most ways, got on like a house on fire. Dave was so protective of Dad, who was beginning to feel his age, and my Dad would not hear a bad word said against Dave.

A boyhood untreated broken bone in his foot saw Dad put into hospital for an operation. His stay was longer than he expected and I do believe that Dave missed his workmate. In the ward with Dad were the usual grumpy, narrow minded old men who criticised everyone and everything. Then one afternoon in came our Dave looking like the wreck of the Hesperus and smiling broadly as he carried in the obligatory bag of grapes. As he trundled down the highly polished ward he shouted "Hello Sid!" The ward mates were shocked and it showed on their disgusted faces. Sid and Dave, the unlikely duo, polished off the grapes and chatted noisily as the intolerant lot looked the other way pretending that they had not seen Dave.

When Dave eventually decided to leave they turned to Dad and said "Who the hell was he?" Dad's simple reply has been a source of pride to me for many years, he said with a touch of affection "That's Dave, he's my mate!"

LEAVE IT OUT, MATE!

Everyone who got involved in the newly flourishing community centre had their own dreams of what they wanted Chats Palace to be. For my part I wanted it to live up the Palace part of the name. I had visions of the wonderful Art Deco Picture Palaces that those of my age had been brought up on, inside this Palace people of all kinds would get together in harmony and respect sharing cultures and skills and producing great events that would show the world what a special place Hackney was. I know that a lot of others shared this dream and I was excited by the talk of equality, socialism, fairness and opportunity for all, well the path to this utopia did not always run smooth.

Nearly all of us who had been raised in Hackney were what we considered to be part of a strong working class culture, a culture with long established unwritten rules and ways of carrying on. These rules were put in place to be fair, respectful and to give everyone a 'crack of the whip'. As you can see we were all sharing the same dreams, but some had their own interpretations of the ways to achieve them.

A good example of this was the practice of 'buying a drink' for a fellow drinker, locals like us follow the unbreakable rule of returning the favour and buying a drink back. This rule evolved to prevent cadgers and ponces from drinking all night without dipping their hands into their pockets and to assure that workers on low wages could drink without running out of money, a natural socialistic and fair system. It also enhanced the buyer's reputation when they asked the bar staff to 'send them a drink over' in a quite loud way safe in the knowledge that the kind gesture would be returned.

Well, a lot of the new incomers to the area had not any knowledge of this practice and took drinks but never returned them giving a lot of us a feeling of being used, causing resentment. Many of us worked in a factory, scrap yard or building site and had to endure being dirty and untidy for most of the day, so we would dress to the nines for our outings. Even a short visit to friends required you to be well turned out, and weekends in the pubs were nothing short of fashion shows for both men and women. However this respectful way of dressing was not observed by many of the people from outside of our culture, they would turn up in scruffy, sometimes worn out clothes. What is more they acted in a what we considered to be selfish way by sitting with their feet on the chairs taking up the precious space while others had to stand, this also had the effect of dirtying our clothing when at last we were able to find a place to park our bums. Personal hygiene was not top of their list, this gave rise to the practice of us calling them 'Soap Dodgers'. This was all very jovial and we got to realise that it was the person inside of the clothes that mattered.

On the other hand they thought that our way of immaculate grooming was ridiculous and would sometimes laugh at us and make disparaging remarks, we managed to take a philosophical view of this irritating behaviour but sometimes someone would step over the bounds of respect.

One particular Saturday a special event was staged and me and my wife arrived looking like Homerton's answer to Brad Pitt and Angelina Jolie, I had treated myself to a very tasty tweed jacket, a silk tie and a tasteful handkerchief that I stuffed rather rakishly in my top pocket. To match the tweed jacket I had chosen a smart pair of light brown suede shoes, I really fancied myself as we made our entrance in our very thought out outfits. Inside the bar we never got the reaction that we wanted, a small group of 'soapy' women sat slurping at a table, one of them got up and stepped in front of us sneering and running her slitty little eyes up and down our sartorial efforts. She was wearing some over sized kind of overalls that had not seen a laundry for many years and she had a sweaty brow and a moist nose, she looked like what my old Sergeant-Major would call 'a bag of shit tied up in the middle with a bit of string'. The sneer on her nasty face grew as she pulled out my tie, removed my pocket handkerchief and blew her snotty nose on it and rubbed her dirty boots over my brand new suede shoes rendering them unfit for my purpose. I was seething and felt my head bursting with thumping rage. No prizes for guessing what I called her and told her that her despicable behaviour was out of order and that if she had been a man she would be picking up her teeth from the floor. I suppose that last sentence would be deemed as being Sexist, so now I am sad that I didn't treat her the same as a man.

Another time I had drawn some cartoons that were used to decorate a programme for one of the pantomimes, a visitor to Chats was being shown around and picked up the programme and was rather patronisingly pronouncing everything was 'fabulous'. He looked at the cartoons and said "these are marvellous, who did them?" Someone said "Brian" and pointed to me. "What, him?" he said in a disbelieving way. All these and many more examples of being looked down at made me aware that prejudice comes in many ways.

All this treatment was getting to me and souring my 'sweet and loving' nature. One day I spoke to a close friend, the very regal Di England, expecting her to sympathise with me but she simply announced that I should stop being silly and ignore these people. "If they cannot accept you for what you are, that is their problem". Just simple logic and wisdom cured my anger. I never quite forgave these people but consoled myself by reasoning that they never knew what a bloody great working class chip I had on my shoulder!

With Di England's counselling tucked in my belt I went forward and saw people in a different way, now it was my turn to be bloody patronising.

SOUND ADVICE

By now I was deeply involved in most of the activities in Chats, running and helping out with a wide range of events along with John Scott, Inky, Ken Parry and our families. We were there just for the fun of it with no particular axe to grind, unlike some users and determined locals, and when at a meeting there was a vote on a crucial issue and we were told that we never had a vote because we were not an affiliated group, the working class chip on our shoulders grew heavier and I'm afraid 'voices were raised'.

After the meeting we had a drink in the bar, still pissed off and feeling underrated. We continued to protest at the injustice of it all when Martin Goodrich, the director of Free Form Arts Trust, came to us and calmed us down by suggesting that we form our own group, with aims and policies. "After all" he said, "It is you lot that help the wheels of Chats Palace to keep moving!" Then he added "Don't underestimate your worth."

It was so obvious, but our anger had blinded our eyes. A meeting was called, officers were elected, if that is the word, and a constitution was drawn up. "What name shall we call ourselves?" Inky asked. John's wife Peggy tutted and said "We are the ones who do all the voluntary work here so let's call ourselves The Homerton Volunteer Community Workers! Now, empowered by our new status and encouraged by Martin's positive comments, we went on to help out with all the events that we did before and to create many of our own, and you know what, we were helped by other groups. Things were looking up for us but we never lost that working class fire in our bellies.

ONWARDS AND ALMOST UPWARDS

The Music Hall shows went from strength to strength, John Scott organised darts tournaments that brought in teams from local pubs throughout Hackney and our events for the under privileged were so successful. All these events encouraged people who would not normally come into such a project as Chats Palace and we think destroyed the suspicions that a lot of locals had about such a liberated venue.

With the re-opening of The Hackney Empire, New Variety spread like wild fire and I had the brilliant idea of combining the best of the New with the cream of Traditional Variety. I was so pleased with myself, why hadn't anybody thought of that before? It can't lose I told myself, I had seen a bit of the new stuff and loved it, jugglers, magicians, even a paper tearer, not much different to the original Old Time Music Hall. All these acts combined with singers and comics from more traditional shows could not help but 'set the place on fire' So with just a slight touch of self importance and arrogance I set out to make a name for myself. Well I did make a name but not one that I care to disclose.

I was working full time at Chats now and had received hundreds of letters appealing to me to book these new artistes into a show and I had a book full of the more established performers, so went ahead with my foolproof plan. Those boyhood dreams of Hollywood were tantalisingly twinkling the lights of Broadway in my brain and I set off planning these shows with ease.

First of all I booked the strength of the entertainment with a strong comic compere and a maestro of a pianist to accompany every act that was about to grace the stage of this downtown Homerton venue. I pored through the applicants without the faintest idea what 'alternative' entertainment really meant. I quite liked the sound of one fine fellow who would perform his own monologue, the very word monologue conjured up memories of childhood visits to The Empire, so I booked him. Then I spoke on the phone to a delightful young woman who described herself as a feminist poet. 'Oooh, lovely' I thought, 'I have always liked Pam Ayres'. A mime artist and an award winning disco dancer were next to be enlisted in the Show to End All Shows. It all came together just a little too easily. I decided to call this extravaganza "The Nut Club" in a flash of nostalgia for a crazy pub event from my boyhood.

 Came the day of the show and I had asked those taking part to arrive in the afternoon to familiarise themselves with Chats, to run through their musical numbers with the pianist and to decide on a running order and they never let me down, except that they all turned up at the same time wanting to tell me their life stories and about their successes in the local church hall.

 The most memorable was the monologuist (if that is a word). He was memorable for his grand, camp, theatrical entrance. The battered doors to the hall swung open as he wafted into 'the auditorium' almost falling over the crates of beer that were being loaded into the bar. What a spectacle he made with his overcoat thrown artistically over his shoulders and a silver topped cane swishing as he walked, on his head he wore an actor's slouch hat that he must have spent many hours getting to sit at the right angle. A fancy waistcoat and a voluminous tie vied for attention with his two-toned co-respondant's shoes. He strolled around the hall soaking in the atmosphere until I spoke to him, he stopped in his tracks, stared at me and raised his carefully placed hat and honoured me with a bow of his head. I wanted to laugh but good manners prevented me. "How dooo you dooo?' he asked and swanned across to the stage where he perched a cheek and spread out his overcoat. "What do you want me to dooo?" he enquired. "What have you got?" I said. "I have just got my own monologue". "Anything else?" "No". I kept a straight face as I said "Well, do that then!"

Next was the delightful feminist poet who wasn't quite as delightful as I thought, she seemed bit reluctant to talk about her poem and simply moped about in a sullen manner. At this stage the Mime artist arrived, he was the one that was delightful, a pleasant young bloke who was thrilled to be with us. I introduced him to our Musical Director, the legendary Tony Locantro, and Tony asked him about his act. "I am going to mime a sword fight with the Invisible Man" said our charming friend. Tony looked excited, and I thought "How boring". "Do you want me to accompany you?" asked our Tony. "Oh no, you can't accompany this, it's too complicated." I saw a twinkle in Tony's eye as he agreed with Monsieur Mime.

At this stage The Champion Disco Dancer arrived. I was expecting some glamorous teenager with suitable glittery garb, but in came a twelve year old girl who was chaperoned by her mum. Now I don't really know how to describe this dancer without being considered a nonce or having the right-on brigade police giving me a visit. She was short, overweight and despite her tender years had an enormous chest that was barely covered by a much too tight T-shirt. She was deemed a champion because she had won a dancing contest in a local youth club, hardly earth-shattering, on reflection I think that they must have let her win just to get rid of her.

For the compere I had booked Harry Dickman, a brilliant actor and comic, I reasoned that if the show started dragging at any time Harry would step in and liven up the proceedings with his sharp wit and crazy humour. I should have been feeling very confident of the outcome of my theatrical efforts, but no, I wasn't!

I had invited all our loyal followers who never missed any Music Hall performance, most were pensioners and members of clubs for more mature punters. There had been a drive to bring in the fans of New Variety and our efforts had paid off. The hall became packed with an unusually mixed audience, lots of our old girls sat side by side with a younger more trendy visitors, they chatted amongst themselves and everyone looked like they were enjoying each others company, I felt good.

   The orchestra (Tony) struck up the overture and Harry ran on with a traditional greeting number, the old faithfuls smiled as they joined in but the newer visitors looked perplexed and uncomfortable. As Harry was doing his warm up performance the mother of the Champion Disco Dancer tugged at my sleeve, "Here, can my girl go on first? She has to be home early, she's only twelve you know." Somehow I managed to get the message to the unflappable Harry and he announced her, then her pre-recorded tape jerked on and the madhouse music began, causing her to throw herself about with abandon. Both her and her oversized frontage seemed to be dancing to different rhythms and within a few short minutes it was all over. The audience didn't know if they should clap or not, so they didn't. Her mum grabbed her, threw a coat at her and they both disappeared out of the door. The dedicated Harry knew that a witty retort was needed to cover the deadly silence that followed the embarrassment that we had just endured, and quick as a flash he said "Thanks for that wonderful act," then turned to the audience and told them "That young lady is studying for her O Levels ... and Ohhh, those levels!" Now this remark would have got a huge laugh in a Carry On film but the followers of the feminist poet sat stoney faced and cleared their throats and shuffled their feet in disapproval.

   After a couple more songs it was time for the feminist poet. Harry announced her and she seemed so surprised to be called upon, I say this because she was comfortably seated in the audience amid her admirers and couldn't decide if Harry had actually invited her to do her bit. After she had made up her mind she laboriously clambered through the seating to eventually reach the stage. Tony played some 'struggling through the audience' music to cover the delay and eventually she began her poem. It became clear that she was definitely not a fan of Pam Ayres and I am sure that Pam Ayres would never be a fan of hers. I suppose that her offering was fit for purpose, but our purpose didn't quite fit her offering. She spoke well with conviction and a touch of anger about the suffering of women, even our faithful old girls were listening to her with a lot of sympathetic nods of the head, but when she spoke of periods, heavy flows and 'abortions in chipped buckets' I'm afraid she lost her newly found fans as the old girls nods turned to frowns and shudders. She received polite applause and a certain amount of admiration.

The act that closed the first half was filled by our very grand monologue author and performer. This strange but fascinating person made his entrance from the back of the hall and sauntered through the audience touching the brim of his stylish hat whenever anyone looked at him. He managed to scramble up on to the stage without losing too much of his dignity and scanned the audience who sat in puzzled silence, a deep breath and he launched into a story of three sisters named Tina, Lena and Meenah. He dramatically strode across the podium as he told us how he rather fancied Tina but she never fancied him, so he then went in pursuit of Lena but with another poor results so then desperately tried his luck with Meenah only to be told to get lost, probably because he was such a boring bastard. After three romantic disappointments his poor old heart broke and he faded away, very sad but did he have to do it in our show?

As he pegged out he dropped even more dramatically onto the front of the stage with his head dangling off of the corner of the platform, the head had a pitiful look upon it's face. Harry announced the interval, the audience trooped out to the bar and our monologue king remained 'dead' on the stage. I went to him to tell him that he could come to life now but he seemed to be enjoying his 'departure' and the rest that it had brought because he never responded to my plea to get off the bloody stage, so I left him there.

The second half opened and everyone crept back to their seats, the orchestra struck up, Harry did a song and a few jokes and a group of us sang a medley of popular songs stepping over the 'corpse' that remained in repose and strangely nobody seemed to care. Now that it was time for Monsieur Mime to silently do his bit so I decided to remove the remains of Tina, Lean and Meenah's unsuccessful suitor. Three of us reverently lifted the 'departed poet' who stayed in character until he was taken into the dressing room as Tony played the Death March. To be honest I was just a little bit relieved when he finally returned to a more earthly world because his post-life acting was quite convincing. Looking back on his unusual performance I get a feeling that he was getting some kind of thrill about being dead, oh well it takes all sorts!

I am pleased to tell you that Monsieur Mime was anything but dead, he was charming, attractive and it felt that we had known him for years and by just walking onto the stage he got a round of applause. He greeted the audience and they were pleased to greet him back, this bloke had something that made us watch every move he made, he was dressed in ordinary street clothes but he was far from ordinary. A brief tale of a duel of honour and he made a grab for his imaginary sword and with anger and passion he swiftly drew it from its scabbard, as this non-existent weapon zipped out of it's non-existent scabbard it made a sound.

Monsieur looked puzzled and cast his gaze onto Tony who sat at the piano with the look of naughty boy on his grinning face, he had simply run his fingers along the keyboard in perfect timing and both him and Monsieur now seemed to be a double act. The duel had now progressed into a full scale swashbuckling combat with every thrust, parry and slash brilliantly brought to life by the impeccable playing of Locantro.

The act received a very enthusiastic ovation and the charming Monsieur shared the accolade with Chats Palace's own maestro who was still smiling so wide that people in the front row needed sunglasses.

Never one to be negative about anything I must say that this show taught me some valuable lessons, the most important one - don't do it again!

GOD BLESS AMERICA!

Along with the other Volunteers, I was now totally committed to our community centre, we all spent many hours and energy devoted to it. Don't run away with the idea that we were making sacrifices to benefit the populace of Hackney, not a bit of it, we were all having great fun and more importantly, getting experience and confidence. We put on some events that we could have only dreamed of. One such stellar occasion was when we managed, through our Music Hall contacts, to bring the whole of the cast of the Muppet Show to our humble hall.

Our contact had managed to get an invitation for us to visit Elstree Studios to have look around and a drink in the bar. We filled a mini-bus with out families and arrived at the studios not sure of what we were there for but we soon found out. As we sat in the bar our contact brought someone over to meet us, it was Leslie Crowther who turned out to be very pleasant but rather tiny and nervy. Then it was the turn for Bob Hoskins to meet us. Bob, who when he was told that we were from bleedin' 'ackney became more cockney and flash by the minute, of course we tried our hardest to beat him at his own game, I'm not sure who won that little game, but it didn't matter, we were loving the unique atmosphere.

Then in walked a young charismatic American bloke who on spotting us came over, he was all smiles and natural charm as he invited us all to have a drink with him. As we sipped away absolutely enchanted with him he casually let it be known that he was 'on the Muppet Team'. "What do you do?" we asked. "I am one of the puppeteers, my name is Richard Hunt. Hey, do you guys want to see the Muppets?"

Did we? What do you think the answer would be? We were all under his spell now and followed him as he led us through many

GOD BLESS AMERICA!

passages and doors until we eventually arrived at the now silent and empty Muppet Workshop. "Here we are" he said proudly and ushered us in.

I am not sure what we were expecting to see but I was filled with a mixture of wonder, a bit of disappointment and just a touch of sadness. The wonder was because the very ordinary workshop was the one that had produced this universally loved show, the disappointment was because, silly old sod that I am, I was looking forward to chatting to all the great stars who we saw on the show every week, and sadness because these brilliant characters were just small toy-like puppets that now that they were off duty, just hung pathetically by the scuffs of their necks on a rusty nail that was knocked into a grubby wall. They all looked so forlorn and somewhat macabre. Like most of the world I had been convinced that Miss Piggy, Kermit and company were somehow really living creatures. That was the magic of the Muppeteers working their artistic spells on all viewers.

One of the puppeteers had been to Chats Palace and seen the Music Hall and simply loved its unique down to earth aura and, to cut a long story short, a performance by all the Muppeteers was arranged.

The Big Night arrived and excitement was lifting us up to level we could never have wished for. Local newspapers had announced that The Muppet Company were coming to Chats, but not many people believed it, but not to worry, the tiny hall was crammed to capacity with friends, neighbours and regulars of Chats, so we had to reserve a place for the Amercan Ambassador and his constant companions (bodyguards, we reckoned).

All the Muppeteers were in the show including the world wide super star, Jim Henson. This founder and producer of the Mighty Muppets, who was a multi-millionaire in many countries was content to melt into the background as he humbly played the drums. With his laid back musician's attitude and his worn in clothes he suited the style of our little venue. Of course there were no puppets but 'The Faces Behind the Muppets' performed good old American Vaudeville in all its transatlantic glory. I am proud to say that Me, John Scott and Ken Parry were invited to do a spot and we sang a medley of American songs with exaggerated Hackney accents.

The event, in the name of the Homerton Volunteers was a fund raiser and our Yankee mates helped us to collect a generous donation to our fund. It was simply a night for Chats Palace to be proud of!

IT MIGHT BE ALRIGHT ON THE NIGHT!

Over the many years that I was involved in Chats Palace I had the privilege to be part of many fine, beautifully produced events, events that took my breath away, that made me want raise my standards to giddy heights. As historically brilliant and perfect as they were, I'm afraid that it is the cock-ups and unplanned occurrences that have stayed longest in my memory.

Chats Palace in spite of our grandiose dreams of palatial splendour remained a 'comfortable' well-worn venue and I suppose that was its appeal, most productions had a low or non existent budget, but no-one noticed, that is until the wheels fell off of the wagon. Ironically these balls ups got the biggest laughs, and added a 'home spun' element to the proceedings, well that's what I tell myself to paper over the cracks.

During one of the Music Hall shows when the magnificent Jim McManus was grabbing the audience by the throat and shaking the laughter out of it, his animated performance became even more animated when a rift appeared in the centre of the stage. Jim, a master of ad-lib, exaggerated the danger as he nervously skipped over the divide giving the gap a withering look and the gap joined in the fun by becoming wider by the minute. By now the chasm was so wide that when Jim put one foot on each side of it there was a danger of him doing the splits and doing himself dire damage to an area of his body that he held dear. The audience was helpless with laughter and Jim's predicament now took on another dimension as the element of danger entered the proceedings, or was it just Jim's superb acting? Whatever it was it had the effect of prompting two blokes from the audience to jump up and push the two halves of the stage back together again much to the relief of the supposedly agitated Jim and the audience who were all big fans of Jim. A big cheer went up for the macho heroes and Jim thanked them and sent a pint to them.

Another time about a dozen of us were crammed onto the very same stage, it was Cockney Night and a newly painted 'cockney' backcloth hung down the back of the 'soap box' stage. We were all singing a free for all Cockney medley led by the pianist, but Alan May the tallest and most conspicuous of us all never knew any of the words so to hide his shortcomings he started acting silly, by pulling faces, shaking his long bony legs in an eccentric manner and cavorting about taking all the attention from us and placing it squarely on himself. Now that he was the centre of attraction he began to enjoy it and attempted a rather gangly pirouette that went out of control sending him into the backcloth and causing him to completely disappear behind the stage. The bloody show-off stole the show that night.

Even the fantastic Pantomimes fell victim to show-stealing balls-ups. In one of the early pantos called 'The Thief of Ragbag' the renowned Dave Fox was gloriously over acting in his part of Mustapha the Miserable. Mustapha was moaning and groaning while sitting on a large

IT MIGHT BE ALRIGHT ON THE NIGHT!

cushion that was placed on a raised dais, under the dais was a lot of the technical gubbins including the pyrotechnics, fireworks to you. One of Mustapha's threats was accentuated by a loud bang and a puff of smoke and the miserable one grumbled on. If he had known that the 'pyro' had started a small fire he might have had something else to moan about but he missed his chance by being completely unaware of the danger of him being barbecued. The audience, who literally had a grandstand view of the threat sat in silence as the small flicker of flame became not so small, the smoke wafted to the ceiling and the red danger licked at the dais. The audience was so entranced by this unscripted addition to the panto that they still sat there without so much of a peep from them, I guess they thought it was part of the act and did not realise the mixture of a crowded hall and an accidental fire was not a marriage made in heaven.

At this point Inky was stirred into action, he simply donned a fireman's helmet, picked up a fire extinguisher and calmly strolled across the stage much to the surprise of a bewildered Mustapha. A blast from the extinguisher quelled the flames and a very smug Inky grinned with self satisfaction and took a bow, the audience went wild!

I will brush lightly over the maniacal technician who thought it was funny to overload the pyro explosions causing chunks of the set to be demolished and lumps of wooden 'shrapnel' to fly across the hall. He also thought it was equally funny to creep into the bar where the punters were drinking and drop a piece of dry ice into their drinks causing their 'wallop' to boil and froth while giving out a dense mist. This bloody overgrown schoolboy whenever he saw me would grab my luxuriant beard and drag my head down to my waist, a humiliating and bleedin' painful experience. He did this many times until my fist making contact with his enormous nose put a stop to his obnoxious habit.

Of course when one of these cock-ups occurred we learned to

make the most of the humour that they generated, like the night when we staged a vaudeville night. Again Jim McManus was compering and from the start the hitches stole the show. We had recently cobbled together front curtains and this was their debut at Chats, As the overture struck up John Scott waited in what passed for the wings and at the given time tugged on the string that opened the 'virgin' curtains. They did part but in a jerky, shaky kind of way helped by Jim tugging at them, this was manna from heaven for Jim whose mastery of world weary attitudes got the audience in stitches.

Us would-be set builders tried to pretend that all this was planned. To close the first half me and Dickie Downes, together with Mike Woods, a banjo player, got together a corny bench in the park spot. I painted a back cloth adorned with a view of Central Park complete with New York skyline and we placed a park bench centre stage. I sat at one end of the bench and Dickie sat at the other, in the middle sat Mike with his feet on the bench and his skinny bum perched on the back rail of the real park bench. At the given signal John Scott nervously tugged at the curtain string and to everyone's relief it opened revealing us trio of would be vaudevillians, Tony Locantro struck up the first notes of a lovely old song called 'Just a little fond affection' and Mike strummed away giving the performance another layer of nostalgia. The audience loved the song and for what it is worth, so did we, all was going swimmingly until at the end of the song both me and Dickie stood up to respond to the rapturous applause. The action of standing up upset the balance of the bench and Mike, his banjo and his skinny bum hurtled backwards crashing to the stage in a way that Norman Wisdom would have envied. The audience went wild and when the sadistic buggers called 'More! More!' Mike got a fit of giggles that stopped us from getting on with the next song.

The next numbers were a 'Moon Medley' and I had made a paper moon complete with a man in the moon face that was to smile rather inanely at the very sporting audience. It was suspended by catgut and would be lowered when needed. With me and Dickie firmly sat on the bench and Mike nervously teetering on the back rail we launched into a catchy version of 'Shine on Harvest Moon'. At the prescribed moment the man in the moon failed to appear so, unsuccessfully trying to look calm, I glared at John who had a concerned look on his face. Using my eyebrows I tried to tell John to sort it out and get that bloody moon on stage, which he did, but one of the catgut strings went awry and when he did arrive the poor old man in the moon spun round so fast it must have made him giddy. Now the boisterous audience were cheering and laughing as they took the Micky out of our efforts to bring Hollywood to Homerton.ABeginclickiergin, in his usual fun filled way, declared "Fuck it, let's have a sing along" and we did what we were good at, getting everyone into a party mood. Strangely, after the show we had so many compliments about this being the funniest show they had seen for ages.

DICKIE

I had known of Dickie Downes for most of my life, as a skinny 16 year old I had sneaked into the Deuragon Arms, a legendary entertainment pub, to see the Sunday morning talent shows. The prize for the winner was a fiver, quite a comfortable sum in those days and Dickie took the prize most of the time and deservedly so. However it wasn't until we got together in Chats Palace that I knew him well.

Dickie was born with a beautiful voice, a cheeky personality and a love of music and art. As a small boy he sang in clubs and halls, he told me once that some of his relatives who were also entertainers and musicians had a small lorry and in the summer they all went to Southend, called into all the pubs and clubs on the way there, did a bit of singing and moved on to the next one. What a way to learn your trade! In his time he had been a market trader, a publican, did a bit of duckin' and divin' and had a bit of business in Soho that we won't mention. He was a true East Ender!

At one time he took over the Deuragon Arms and converted it into a theatre. Most of the entertainment was the best of Pub Variety bringing in punters and performers from all over London and further afield. The Deu' as it was known as, had a history of gay entertainment even back to the days before the word Gay was thought up and transvestites and non-straight people flocked to the pub mingling happily with locals.

Dickie made sure that this tradition carried on ensuring that the entertainment remained the best in London. However, it was Dickie who was the main draw.

When he came to Chats he brought with him his talent and experience, he could sing, strum a banjo, dance a bit of tap and soft shoe, and had a vast knowledge of all kinds of music and songs.

DICKIE

Strangely, in spite of his experience he suffered from stage nerves. He blotted out his anxiety by drinking a lot before a performance. It was never a problem, he never misbehaved, but the silly sod could forget things. Like once when he was to do a song and dance routine he was immaculate in his stage costume, looked wonderful, but forgot to remove his glasses and don his tap shoes - he only realised this when he started tapping and no noise was heard. This did not spoil the pleasurable act because Dickie's warm, sparkling personality overcame the lack of taps and his voice thrilled the audience.

Far from being a tough aggressive bloke, he was sensitive and emotional. A good song or singer could move him to tears and once when I was asked to paint a backcloth for a local group and Dickie came with me to 'keep me company' he was even moved by my rather crude depiction of an East End street.

We became firm friends and performed many a show together and when I asked him to take part in the first Variety show at the newly opened Hackney Empire, guess what? He cried.

With his lovely wife Eileen he took over the bar at Chats Palace and brought a professional touch to it, something that had been lacking before.

I miss him, and Eileen, and the cheeky twinkle that he had.

THE PROFESSOR

Professor Tommy Shand! The very mention of his name makes me feel happily nostalgic. He was a mixture of hilarity and pathos, a strange but appealing figure who had strong likeness to Charlie Chaplin except that he never tried to impersonate Chaplin, he was what he was. One look at him brought feelings of silent movies and Victorian Music Hall and made you smile and feel warm about him.

I don't know much about his beginnings, he mentioned that he once had a wife and had served in the army, no more details were forthcoming, well he wasn't one to chat at length about anything. This only led to his air of anonymity being part of his special personality, you could simply take him for what you saw of him, if you needed to probe further he just ignored the questions as if he had never heard them without you even noticing it.

He did tell me that while in the army he was a military musician learning to play many instruments. I assume that his multi-instrumental skills prompted him to form his unique act.

I was about to say that his act was timeless but that is not really true, there definitely was a touch of bygone days about it, what I meant to say is that people of all ages liked it. It was a multi-instrumental act with a large dollop of eccentricity and inventiveness about it, for instance he had a trumpet with a typewriter keyboard, a clarinet with a doorbell, a saxophone with a multitude of clips and pipes covering it, a pistol, a swannee whistle and a squeaky fiddle, amongst other peculiar paraphernalia. He always wore a bowler hat and a tail coat which only confirmed his Chaplinesque appearance.

He would arrive on stage with a look of bewilderment about him and hesitantly select his first instrument of torture (as he called them). It was usually his trumpet and he would announce that he was about to play 'Smoke Gets in Your Eyes'. With a large puff of his cheeks a cloud of smoke blew out of the horn covering the first two rows of the audience. Then a corny joke or two and straight into a jazzy number on the clarinet with liberal amounts of dings on the doorbell, and another piece on his trumpet that finished with him writing a letter of complaint on the built in typewriter that finished with another ding and a sheet of paper shooting out of the crazy apparatus and him catching it in mid air with perfect timing. By now the audience were hanging on to every note and every move that he made, so he would pick up his creaky violin, put a handkerchief on his right shoulder and then put the fiddle on his left shoulder and announce his well-chosen number. Now, the piece of music was called Brahm's Hungarian Dance No.5 in G minor, but Tommy disgracefully reduced it to 'The Oi Song'. The fiddle led the vigorous classic and at the end of each line of music Tommy encouraged the happy crowd to shout 'Oi'! Of course they never needed too much encouragement, in fact they often carried on 'Oi-ing' after the number was over.

He finished his nutty performance with a the most hilarious, riotous number that verged on vulgarity if your mind moved in those circles. He picked up the battered old saxophone, you know, the one with all the clips and elastic bands. The yards of pipes that snaked their way around the instrument and the very look of the shabby 'machinery' of this highly unusual object made the audience giggle and wonder what kind of mayhem lay ahead.

Tommy now put on a serious face and started to play in a sincere way, the number was the old classic, 'I'm in the Mood for Love'. The silent punters waited for something to happen and it did, just as they were getting lulled by the plaintive music something could be seen slowly poking out of the horn of the sax. As it grew it was clear that it was a balloon, a long red balloon that grew and grew with every puff that our crazy Tommy sent along the pipes and you would have to be dense if you didn't get the significance of the 'In the Mood' music and the large phallic object that was growing by the minute. At this point Tommy's usually expressionless face acquired a lecherous look that he applied to any group of females who had the stupidity to sit near the front, of course they would be helpless with near hysteria and if, when Tommy leaned from the stage and poked the giant dildo at them, they made a vain effort to get out of reach Tommy would leap from the stage and chase them around the hall. All good almost clean fun!

    This extraordinary, well thought out act went very well, that is until something went awry. Sometimes one of the elastic bands would snap or the clips would become unclipped or one of the many pipes sprang a leak, then the immaculate timing was not on time, the phallic wonder failed to throb threateningly or the smoke refused to leave the trumpet. It was then that the dear old professor simply put on his most pathetic face and played a selection of old favourites.

    His sad looks could move strong men to tears, once when I was in Rathbone Market in Canning Town I thought that I could hear the haunting strains of an old song, "That sounds like Tommy" I said to myself and it was. A lump came to my throat as I caught sight of him standing in a forlorn corner of the market, he was busking. He looked so shabby and sad as he weakly puffed at his faithful old saxophone, and his cap that was placed in front of him was empty. He deserved more than that.

    But I have another, better memory of him to keep in my heart. I booked him to entertain at The Hackney Marsh Fun Festival on Daubeney Fields and he asked me "What do you want me to do?" "Just go out on the field and enjoy yourself" I replied. Being preoccupied I forgot about him until later in the day when I spotted him skipping between the stalls, sax in hand and playing 'The Teddy Bear's Picnic' with a long line of small kids happily skipping along behind him. Thank You Professor!

I'M NOT WELL!

George Williams, who was a firm favourite at Chats Palace, was a comic with a gimmick, his gimmick was that he was hilariously funny. His act was well honed and superbly performed but it was George himself who provoked howls of laughter. He also had a life story that could be made into a film, so perhaps I will start this tale at the beginning.

George was born in 1910 in Liverpool, when he was 4 years old the family moved to Nottingham and there George acquired the accent that stayed with him all his life. He was a fragile, weedy child, a look that would never leave him but would shape his life and provide him with the basis of fame and fortune when he used the sickly look in his act.

As a small child he took part in a Sunday School show and was asked to sing a hymn, but when he stepped forward to sing his nerves caused him to forget the words, so not to disappoint the large audience he sang a popular song of the time "Daddy wouldn't buy me a Bow-wow". His sad face and stick-thin body moved the audience and sowed the seeds of a lifetime in the theatre. By the late 30s he was very well known and sought after Variety performer, and when war was declared George, who was a Quaker and as such was opposed to violence, volunteered for the Fire Service. He was also an ENSA member and carried on his comedy act all over Britain entertaining the armed forces.

He once told me a lovely little wartime story that still makes me smile. He was now famous and his funny little face was familiar to everyone. One night when he was topping the bill at our own Hackney Empire he left the stage door and stepped out into the darkness of the black-out carrying his suitcase. Suddenly the flash of a torch blinded him and two coppers gazed at him with suspicion. "What have you got in that case?" they asked, as if he might be a Nazi collaborator. "Ohhh, that" whined George, "That is my costume".

Now the cops were even more suspicious, "What do you mean, costume?" they quizzed. George opened the case to reveal a drab suit that did nothing to pacify the zealous coppers, so George explained that he was 'George Williams who was topping the bill at the Empire'. A look of disbelief ran across their faces as they said "You don't look like George Williams, how can you prove it?" George rummaged deeper into his case and fetched out a familiar flat cap that he perched upon his dainty head, then putting on his pathetic, pitiful 'stage face' said "How about this then?" The two officers' faces lit up as they said "It is you George! Can we have an autograph?"

His act, that was unique, always started with the compere introducing him as something special for the ladies as he fetched George on - and with a burst from the band there he stood, about 6 stone of fragile, reedy, sickly manhood complete with his ill-fitting suit, a funny little flat cap, a long scarf that wound around his scrawny neck and dangled to the floor and a flour-white face.

The audience would burst out laughing as George stood stock still, causing even more laughter, the longer that he stood motionless the more the crowds cried with laughter. Eventually he would quietly explain "I'm not well!", causing yet even more hysteria, then he would look at the audience and gently ask "Have you ever had that going off feeling coming on?" Then he would limp through his string of jokes that were all about illness, weakness, death and dying and funerals. It never failed.

 Quite rightly he was propelled to fame and what we call today Super-Stardom. His life and career could not have been better when the outmoded attitudes of those days shattered him and heaped misfortune and suffering upon him. He was found guilty of 'committing a homosexual act' and was sentenced to two years in prison. He served his time but when he returned to his theatrical life he was not wanted and his work dried up. What is even more galling was that another comic was using his act and reaping the rewards of it.

Then in the 1980s, fringe theatre allowed him to perform his act again, attitudes had changed and no-one cared what your sexual preferences were. Our old mate Jim McManus brought him to Chats Palace and immediately there was a mutual admiration between George and Chats.

Old age was upon him now but it never affected him or his ability to create mirth. He lost his hearing and when I phoned him he could not hear my requests so all our communications were done by old fashioned mail. When he was performing he could not hear the laughter, a problem that would have defeated lesser comics by ruining their timing, but the undefeated George simply said "Oooh, it's easy! I just wait until I can see that they are not moving and then tell the next joke."

Age never stood a chance against this special man. In his 84th year he took part in a show at the Sebright Arms, Hackney Road, a show that was recorded by the BBC. The Sebright was usually well attended but on this night it was 'standing room only and then squeeze in a bit more'. Many nurses and doctors from the next door Children's Hospital and many regulars crammed in and when George appeared on stage there was a surge forward with the unfortunates at the back having to stand on the tables to see this comedy legend. Dear old George didn't let them down and there were cheers, and laughter at every joke as the younger generation had a glimpse of traditional variety at its very best. George smiled sweetly as praise was piled upon him, the people doing the praising not knowing that George never heard a word of it.

The following year we all took part in a show at Finsbury Park that boasted Britain's oldest and youngest comics, on the bill was George Williams and a very young up and coming bloke called Lee Evans.

Soon after, George slipped away in his sleep, he was 85 and at last his 'not well' status caught up with him. In spite of his years, his diary was full of bookings.

Once he asked me to dinner at his sumptuous flat in South London and he showed me some of the many oil paintings that he had done, they were all of Music Hall Artistes and theatres and I was deeply flattered by him taking one from the wall and presenting it to me because I was 'a special friend'. Over the years I have boasted to fellow performers that I had one of The Wonderful George Williams paintings only to be told many times "Yes he gave me one too".

GEORGE WILLIAMS
1910 - 1995

"OF ALL THE COMMUNITY CENTRES IN THE WORLD ..."

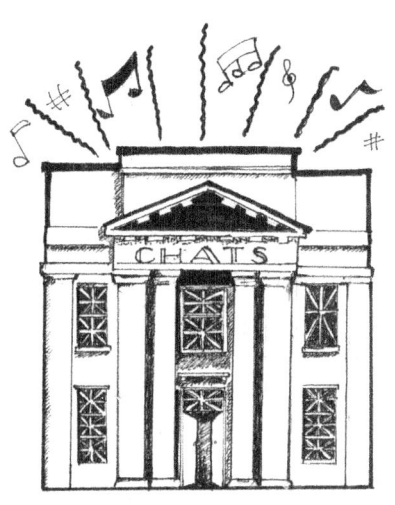

From reading the tales so far anyone would think that Chats Palace was solely involved in Music Hall and Variety but this was far from the truth. Of course I have been telling my side of the story without so much as a mention of the many groups, individuals and users who also took advantage of what was offered by this very successful Community centre.

Chats boasted an extremely varied choice of facilities, from a crèche to a senior citizens club. Jazz, classical music, reggae, punk, rock n' roll, opera, blues and so many more music forms filled the building bringing with them a wide cross section of people who just simply loved music. The result of this was that anyone with an open mind could learn from and enjoy things that they had previously known nothing about.

Music workshops were set up giving local musicians the encouragement that was not available elsewhere, quite a few locals went on to have careers in music and some found fame.

There was a Caribbean Supplementary School, a poets group, an advice session, art workshops, dance workshops, photographic workshops and so many more that my now ancient memory has let slip by. The hall has seen some strange, weird and wonderful and some very satisfying evenings. Of course it is the weird and wonderful that you want to hear about, like the Friday Night that I was on duty looking after the hall and controlling the crowd that on this particular night numbered about five or six very young teenagers. Friday nights at that time were when bands, singers and musicians could stage their own entertainment, so we never knew what to expect until it arrived. On this particular night the hall had been booked by a musician from 'up north' who promised a new form of 'band' performance, this was the future he prophesied. Our sound and lighting operator stood by in puzzled expectation as the Rock Star styled bloke entered the hall. Well he was right, it was something unusual for that time but we had heard of it, don't get too excited, it was - Backing Tapes!

When all was set up and the doors opened the surge of the five youngsters looked a bit puzzled and surprised to see a solitary soul stood on the stage in place of the usual frantic crowd of artistes and all their kit. The one man band was a rather skinny bloke who obviously was a fan of the many chart toppers of the time, he was dressed in a tight fitting black outfit and he had the shirt opened down to his waist showing off a chest that deserved to be covered up.

The backing tape thumped out a constant rhythm and he started singing. The entire audience felt disappointed, all five of them, but he gallantly thumped on trying his best to incite the 'crowd' to get involved in the rather dull music. The entire audience sat at the back of the hall with blank expressions on their faces, sucking soft drinks through a straw. If only they knew what was about to liven up this odd night they would have ordered something a bit stronger.

About an hour into the tedious gig the double doors crashed open and in burst a very overweight, strange looking bloke who was dressed in a grey boiler suit and had shaven head. He sauntered around the almost empty hall as if he owned it watched by the dozen or so admirers that had entered with him, then walked up to the one man band and stared at him in a superior way, and started mimicking his moves but with much more success. I know it was a bit cruel

"OF ALL THE COMMUNITY CENTRES IN THE WORLD ..."

to do so, but I laughed so much that my body ached and my vain attempts to keep a straight face only made the ache more intensely. At this stage he jumped onto the stage and moved about in a hilarious take off of the poor sod who was supposed to be the main attraction and suddenly he opened his enormous mouth and a gigantic tongue emerged and dangled somewhere south of his chin. By now the audience, all five of them remember, were so worked up and excited that I considered dialling 999 and our audacious gatecrasher announced that his band were to be at Chats Palace soon and they would 'tear the place apart', well they had done a pretty good job of this week's star.

The cheeky, ungracious, anarchic unwanted guest brought with him the best entertainment we had seen for a long time and he wasn't even trying. He held court in the bar, being just as manic as he had been in the hall so I thought that I would speak to him. "Just who are you?" I asked as if it was really me who owned the place. "Me? I'm Buster Bloodvessel, and my band is called Bad Manners, and soon everyone will know of us."

I am so pleased that Buster had given us the opportunity to know him before anybody else.

In the 1980s when Johnny Rotten and the Sex Pistols led the punk revolution the national press had a field day by telling the British public of the threat to civilisation that 'these unwashed, anarchic, drug laden disrespectful' youths were. Of course, the British public went along with this nonsense leading to them being vilified and even feared, so when a group of fans of a certain band booked the hall there was, I am ashamed to say, a bit of apprehension. A number of Chats Palace members came along to defend their beloved centre from the onslaught of ill mannered, destructive Punks. In came the punks dressed in black bin bags held together with safety pins, straps, and studs. Some of them had shabby clothing, but a close look at these clothes revealed that the shabbiness was the result of many hours of preparation and the strange hair styles must have taken hours in front of the mirror. I was intrigued and described them as 'Walking Works of Art'. The band struck up and the works of arts couldn't wait to get on to the dance floor and as strange as it seemed to us 'stuck in the past' fossils, they put their hearts and souls into it enjoying every move. At 11o'clock they finished on the dot as promised and these 'children of destruction' set to sweeping the hall, wiping the tables and stacking the chairs. A couple of them came to us to apologise for breaking a couple of glasses and to offer to pay for them. We learned two important lessons from this amiable event, one was to never judge a book by its cover and two, don't believe the crap that the gutter press spouts!

All this was in stark contrast to another event, this event was a performance put on to fund-raise for the local Labour Party, a cause that we were all eager to support. Memories of exactly what the performance was have been buried under deep, heavy memories of the disrespectful actions of the people who turned up. Chairs and tables were laid out to accommodate the so called audience who instead of watching the performers talked, shouted, argued and generally behaved like hooligans. After 20 minutes or so the audience ceased to exist and a mob of ill mannered arseholes had taken their place spreading themselves to every corner of the building where they guzzled vast amounts of real ale! By the end of the evening the place looked like a bomb had landed on it and one nutter was banging his head against the wall refusing to leave the bar. Of course the inevitable puddles of vomit were donated and one dirty bastard had even pissed in the hall. I felt ashamed and disappointed with these individuals who were supposed to be representing the workers of Britain.

UNITY IS STRENGTH!

Chats Palace, quite rightly, had a reputation for being very left wing, a reputation that was lived up to by its support for many causes. These were the days of Maggie Thatcher and her drastic policies, most of which seemed to be to punish working people and to destroy their champions, the Trade Unions. The word 'community' was disapproved of, I think because it smacked of the strength of united people, this attitude was well and truly opposed by all and this is where Chats Palace lent support to many groups who were determined to stand firm against what they saw as an assault on socialism.

The building provided help with fund raising, protest and publicity for those who needed it.

Groups like Rock Against Racism, Troops Out, Support the Unions and many more held fund raising gigs on a regular basis. Local schools and even a church used the workshops to produce banners and posters and many meetings were held.

When the Fire Brigade went on strike it was a long and bitter struggle which led to the government stopping payments and to the union running out of strike pay, fund raisers were staged and the good old London public kept the strike going by filling the firefighters' buckets with cash in the local shopping centres. But it was the historic Miners' strike that still stays in the mind and angers it's supporters to this day. Pickets were stationed all over Britain including Hackney, the huge power station at Millfields was still in operation at the time, consuming tons of coal. A group of Welsh miners set up a picket outside the gates, this post stayed for the best part of a year with the miners becoming part of the local community, collections were held in most of the local pubs and clubs but it was Chats Palace that became the meeting place an almost the second home for the strikers. Many events were held to raise money and to pay tribute to them including Rock Concerts, folk evenings, a pantomime performance and not to be left out, a Music Hall Show. At this show a large part of the audience were Welsh so we decided to give it a Cambrian theme. Both me and John Scott, the very cockney Plastic Pearlies, had Welsh mums and all my uncles were miners so we knew one or two Welsh words and songs. We struggled through one song trying our best to fool the audience into thinking that we knew exactly what the strange sounds really meant. As you might have guessed it never fooled our Welsh brothers and sisters but the rest of them were very impressed. We finished the show with a popular, rather sentimental song about Wales, we sang 'We'll keep a Welcome in the Hillside'. As the first note was played every Welshman in the audience sprang to their feet and sang with patriotic fervour, both me and John stood in proud silence. The rest of the right-on audience, who were not usually in favour of shows of patriotism, stood up as a sign of solidarity with their Welsh comrades.

    The result of the strike, a crushing defeat for the pitmen brought sorrow and anger to all involved. Maggie and her henchmen had battered their way to victory and now it was time for our close friends from Wales to depart, never one to control my emotions I kept my farewells brief as they walked out of the door for the last time, but my efforts were in vain as I watched Rene Rice, one of the staunchest of supporters, tearfully embrace the saddened band of colliers. Cymru am Byth.

A BIT DIFFERENT

I have always been fascinated by people who dare to be different. In this world full of 'clones' who dress and think just like everyone else, the sight of someone dressed flamboyantly brightens my day. When the New Romantics were fashionable and we saw young people going about their business wearing knee breeches, feathered hats and yards of lace I looked at them with envy and even the much reviled Punks got my admiration by simply not caring what the great British public thought of them and their adventurous style.

One day when I was signwriting a pub in Holloway someone walked up behind me and admired my work, when I turned round there standing before me, as bold as brass was … Buffalo Bill! An elegant well spoken man was dressed just like our western hero, right down to his famous beard and flowing moustache, he looked wonderful and was obviously living out a schoolboy dream. I just wished that I could lose my inhibitions and do what he was doing.

As a young boy in Whitechapel I studied the bohemian characters that flaunted themselves along the streets and without any doubt the ones that captured my imagination were the 'Nancy Boys'. This was not a derogatory name but a means of describing men who dressed as women to entertain and couldn't give a monkey's what was said about them. Of course they were gay men and proud of it, and were very comfortable with what they were and had no fear of displaying the fact. In the street markets you could sometimes see them singing and dancing as they performed their very camp acts for an enthusiastic audience. Of course, at that time being gay was not an advantage, in fact homosexual acts were a crime and we were all brought up to 'be careful' of such people and to 'keep your back to the wall', but in spite of the prejudice of the time the more outrageous nancies became East End celebrities who lit up the otherwise drab streets.

Perhaps the most noted of them was the legendary Diamond Lil, an extremely popular and well known figure who could always be seen trolling along Whitechapel Road, Bethnal Green Road and Shoreditch High Street. Lil ambled along as if lit by some internal light that radiated from him, it was like a beacon that attracted everyone's eyes to soak up his glorious appearance. He was immaculately dressed in a tailored suit or overcoat and a crisp white shirt complete with a tastefully flamboyant tie, he had a natural poise that showed off his sartorial efforts, all very masculine, but then he added a large flower in his buttonhole and sparkling jewelry to his lapels. This display was topped, as only Lil could do, by his carefully applied make up and bright bleached blond hair that was finger waved giving him the look of a silent film beauty. No-one could pass him without calling " Hello Lil" or honking a car horn, both men and women flocked around him shaking his hand, embracing him or even kissing him. Some of the more villainous hard men would kiss him in public, a sure sign that they didn't give a monkey's what people thought either.

Another equally celebrated queen was the marvellous Gaye Travers, a glamorous entertainer in the style of the original Nancy Boys. Gaye compered at the Deuragon Arms for years drawing in many powdered and primped effeminate men. I loved the fact that they decorated the streets around Homerton whenever they trotted along to this unique pub.

I know that I said that I liked being with people who were different but Blimey I never guessed that I would be involved with some of the most fascinating and intriguing characters that I once would have only dreamed of. I was now performing at Brick Lane Music Hall on a regular basis and got to work with some of the greatest Gay icons of that age, including the one and only Danny La Rue. Danny's story is well known so I will concentrate on some of the others. I have three stars of the gay scene to tell you about, all are now no longer with us but the legends live on in memories and conversations. They are Phil Starr, Tommy Osbourne and the glorious Dockyard Doris.

Before I start, let's explain the workings of Camp etiquette and procedures. All these personalities are of course men who portray female characters, not always on the stage, so I will have to tell you that they all have birth names and camp stage names and there are loose, unwritten rules about addressing them. Sometimes I will use their given name or maybe their camp name, and sometimes I may refer to them as 'he' or 'she', so keep on your toes and don't get confused.

PHIL STARR. I was aware of Phil, or Phylis, many years ago and I think that I may have seen him/her then. He was without any doubt one of the funniest people I have known, not just on stage but in 'real life'. He was a slim insignificant looking bloke with a long, kind face, someone who you may not have noticed if you passed him on the street, but as soon as he stepped onto the stage he became Phylis. In all her gorgeous finery and make up she produced gasps from the audience. She had a lovely pair of shapely, long legs, a fabulously slim figure with all her 'bits and pieces' neatly tucked away and topping all this was her long, kind but naughty face that was surrounded by a eye-popping hairdo. As soon as she opened her mouth out came this nasal voice that caused the punters to laugh uncontrollably and to continue all through her many stories about her 'old man', traffic wardens, little nuns, ugly birds, indecent phone calls and many more situations all in his nasal drawling voice. Most of these stories were naughty, vulgar or downright filthy, but all of them were hilarious causing the audience to fall about. It never mattered if the same stories were told over and over again because they had the same effect as they did when first heard, in fact I was witness to something that seems strange now, if she left out one of her best jokes the audience would call out for it, just as though they were calling for their favourite song. When Phylis obliged and retold the joke her ardent admirers would repeat it word for word as she went along and when it came to the punch-line they laughed and cheered as if they had never heard them before.

My abiding memory of the magnificent Phylis is sharing a few pantos with her. When she played the Wicked Queen and appeared through a burst of smoke, with a strange look on her face would announce "Poof!"

TOMMY OSBOURNE. Once again I had heard the name Tommy Osbourne bandied about in conversation but having never met him I could not get interested in him. Our first meeting was a bit uncomfortable, I was in the Sebright Arms in Hackney Road to watch the Music Hall show, the place was packed as usual with punters jostling for a good view of the performance, across the room I saw a very attractive, tastefully dressed woman. What made me uncomfortable was the fact that this woman was staring straight at me and smiling as if she was pleased with what she saw, I supposed I was just a bit flattered but never being a philanderer I moved over to the bar out of the gaze of this femme fatale. But when I looked again the trollop was still staring and smiling in what I thought was a seductive way, so now I felt that there was a slight trace of creepiness about this situation. When the interval came I sought the refuge of the dressing room and my mate Laurence Payne, "What's up with you?" he asked in his usual mocking manner. I told him about my stalker and he got just a bit excited, he's funny that way, "Let's have a look at her" he urged. I pointed her out and now he really was excited as he grinned like a donkey on heat. Then quoting that well known Music Hall joke he said "That's no lady, that's Tommy Osbourne!" Well you can guess how stupid I felt, but I wasn't going to take the blame for my idiocy. "Fancy walking about like that, the flash old cow" I bitterly replied.

Looking back on the incident I should have introduced myself to Ms. Osbourne and then I would have learned that Tommy wasn't staring at me but that she had very bad eyes and was simply staring into a blurry space, and that the fetching smiles were just Tommy's natural happiness. Nevertheless I wasn't enamoured by her for leading me on.

A short time later we came face to face when we were both in a Pantomime together. At the first rehearsal we chatted like old mates and surprisingly we liked each other. I always seemed to be cast as the villain, probably because I was the only butch bloke in the theatre, and Tommy was always the Dame, what else? At the end of nearly every Panto the baddy and the dame inevitably get married, so me and Tommy got hitched a thousand times or more, so any differences between us were now ancient history.

As well as performing in Music Hall and Panto, I looked after the charitable shows that we took out to clubs, homes, hospitals and so on and it seemed sensible to ask Tommy to accompany me. He was pleased that I had asked him and we made a good team along with Michael Topping on the piano. Old Topping was another dyed-in-the-wool queen and fitted well into our nomadic troupe.

I suppose at this stage I should explain that Tommy was not just a queen but a good old fashioned transvestite, he loved to dress in women's clobber all the time and what is more had a fine sense of style. In the early days of us working together he wore clothes that were androgynous, you know, slacks, slip on shoes, blouse-like shirts and nice light jackets and certainly not a scrap of make-up. He would take his frocks and make-up and prepare for his appearance when we arrived at the venue.

I was in the habit of picking Tommy up from his flat in Clerkenwell when we worked together, I would press the intercom and wait for him to come out, all the time watching out for the traffic warden. On this particular day I buzzed the intercom and waited in the van aware that the 'yellow peril' was dangerously near when a woman came out of the door, because I had one eye on the pavement I never took much notice of her, but where was Tommy? The woman approached the van and said "Hello Dear, you're on time as usual." It was Tommy, and I was for some reason, pleased to see that he was completely dressed in women's clothes. His face was finely made up and he had a blonde hairdo, tasteful ear rings, fashionable sun glasses, a bright red fitted jacket, tailored black slacks and high heeled shoes. Without any compulsion I simply said "Tommy, you look so good". He smiled and looked so pleased with me, then I realised why I also felt so pleased, it was because we were both comfortable with him being a transvestite. From then on he always wore female attire so it is time for me to refer to him as her and to use her camp name, Dolly. Are you keeping up with me?

At this stage I will tell you what I know about Tommy, oops! sorry Dolly. She was born in Covent Garden where her Dad was a banana merchant in the old fruit market. She went to a local Catholic school where one of her classmates was Danny La Rue, they remained life long friends, and it is no surprise that they both became performers. Dolly was a 'good looking woman' who at the age of eighteen entered a beauty contest, it was for the title of Miss Margate and when she lined up with all the female beauties she came third.

A lot of drag artists and transvestites are effeminate but not Dolly, she was naturally feminine and took much effort to stay that way.

When we both arrived a one of our venues we were often asked if we were married, of course the very butch me got just a bit flustered and made sure that they knew that I was married to a lovely lady and that I had a large family. This only led to many questions about Dolly and our relationship, so very tongue-in-cheek we would say yes we are married, after all we had been 'married' many times in Pantoland. Of course there was a lot of micky taking, whenever I entered the dressing room at Brick Lane Music Hall the very laconic

A BIT DIFFERENT

Phil Starr often said in his distinctive way "Oh Blimey, here comes Dolly's old man". Once when we were performing in a hospital and Dolly and me were singing a duet there was a pair of flash old birds sitting in the front row. I stepped forward to sing a solo part when one of the dodgy pair eyed up my beardy manliness, nudged her mate and said in a loud voice "Look at the fucking state of that!" Dolly immediately stepped forward, stared at the mouthy one with indignation and said "Do you mind missus? That's my old man you are talking about", as she gave her a most withering stare. That well and truly shut her up.

Another time when we were returning from Southend after another performance my trusty old van came to a juddering halt and refused to start again. Dolly looked concerned but I had spotted a yard full of vans about half a mile away so I walked back and asked for help, the owner very kindly tried to start it without success so towed the van back to his yard and said that he would look after it for me. Dolly sat in the front seat looking like Bethnal Green's answer to Zsa Zsa Gabor and I kept her abreast of the situation, but silly sod that I am, I kept calling her Tommy or even Tom. Of course this caused suspicions amongst the workers in the yard, so we had a stream of callers to the cab of the van just to look at this woman called ... 'Tom?' When they had worked out just what was what, some of the blokes wanted to talk to Dolly and to marvel at her glamour and some could not look her in the eye but found pressing matters that took them to other parts of the yard. I called a cab and on the way back home she called me all sorts of names for revealing her secret. We returned to my place and Dolly and my wife caught up on all the gossip. Pam complimented Dolly on her appearance and they both disappeared to the bedroom and Pam's vast collection of dresses and shoes and talked for ages about fashion and style leaving me to reflect on my unthoughtful faux pas in the van yard. There was a great mutual admiration and affection between my two 'wives'.

Dolly had a naturally sweet nature and man, woman or inbetween Tommy was the nicest person that I knew.

Living with Dolly was May, an ancient cockney woman who was known to everyone as Auntie May. What an odd couple they made, Dolly dressed up like a Christmas tree and Auntie May completely bereft of glamour, but with a fine command of fruit market bad language, which she used just whenever she wanted to. I was fascinated by Auntie May as I am sure Charles Dickens would have been because I felt that he would have included her in one of his atmospheric novels. Auntie May was in her 90s with a well worn, weather beaten look that only outdoor workers, gypsies and field workers had before face creams were available, her many creases and wrinkles only made her more fascinating. Her hair had never seen even a splash of dye and was a yellowed grey, she simply brushed it straight back across her head where it took on flattened natural waves, she should have been an artist's model. Although she was still mobile she needed the help of a battered old push chair to keep her balance and as she aged a stoop in her back progress into a 45 degree bend. When she sat in the theatre surrounded by people with huge theatrical egos and over the top behaviour she silently sat there with a look of 'seen it all before' on her very straight face. We never did find out if Auntie May was related to Dolly, but it was obvious that they were very close.

DOCKYARD DORIS. Now you may recall that I said that I like people who dare to be different, well I wish now that I had curbed my boastful mouth. Here is the tale of some-one who was even different to the people who are different, if you get my drift. Let me start at the beginning.

Before he founded the fabulous Brick Lane Music Hall, Vincent Hayes opened a small pub, The Lord Hood, in Bethnal Green. In the 'Hood' he staged Music Hall nights with the performers standing on

A BIT DIFFERENT

little more than a soap box with ideas above its station, but in spite of the lack of space the atmosphere was wonderful. I went there with my mate Inky at least once a week. One particular night I felt a bit peckish and went to the tiny food display cabinet that was squeezed onto the end of the bar, behind the bar was a large, round bloke dressed in chef's whites. I politely asked "Is there anything to eat?" The large lump looked at me and rolled his eyes around his head, tutted and gave a deep exaggerated sigh. "There is only that one pie left" he said impatiently, "Do you want it or not?" he said even more impatiently, so after consideration I told him where to stick it. He slammed the cabinet shut and disappeared into the back of the bar. That was my first introduction to Colin Devereux who just happened to be the legend that was Dockyard Doris.

A few weeks later Doris appeared at the Hood, I was looking forward to seeing her as I had heard so much about her but as she came into view both Inky and me realised who it was. "It's that rude git that was here the other week" said Inky. Yes it was, so we were not in the best of moods to enjoy anything that she gave us on that historic night, but within minutes Doris's larger than life personality and her talent won us over. I had seen many drag acts in my time, most of them trying their best to look like a woman, but that was not Doris's style. There standing on the fragile stage was a 20 stone lump of vulgarity who was obviously a burly bloke in women's clothing. Her almost circular face was filled with naughtiness and the hint of danger, she looked just like she had stepped down from a seaside postcard and that was her appeal. She sang that old Music Hall song 'Don't have any more, Mrs. Moore', a song that I had heard and sung many times, but it was Doris's cheeky delivery of this ordinary song that made me realise that it was in fact quite a rude number. From then on I was in her fan club.

Within a few months we were both working together as Brick Lane Music Hall was being created, it was then that I discovered

Colin and Doris were two different people, not literally of course, but in personality. Colin was asked to answer the phone to take potential bookings and to talk up the yet to be opened theatre, but his niggly, surly attitude caused Vincent to give him a talking to and to accuse him of having 'tension in his voice', a phrase that was echoed many times by many of the workers until he blew his top at full volume.

Colin could be awkward, cantankerous and sometimes exasperating, he often found fault with anything that was done for him. If we were doing a gig together I would offer to pick him up and take him to the venue, he would sigh and reply "If you want" as if he was doing me a favour. When I arrived at his flat he would open the door with a face like a smacked arse and I would say in an exaggerated way "Hello Darling". "Don't call me Darling" he would reply. "Why not Darling?" I would ask. "Because I don't want the neighbours to know that I am gay!" was his answer. He would then proceed to mince across the grounds of the flats in the campest manner that I have ever seen. Of course I was left to struggle along behind him carrying his many costume and wigs like some old lackey and when I carefully placed them in the back of the van he would bark "Mind my bloody wigs!" The journey was livened up by his constant criticism of my driving, the route that I had taken and how much he wished that he had taken the bus. On arrival at the venue he would crash into the dressing room mumbling and cursing. In fact he was a real pain in the pudding.

However as soon as Doris's make-up was applied Colin evaporated into thin air and there was the loving Doris holding my hand, fluttering her three inch eyelashes and whispering softly "I'm sorry that I was rude to you, you know that I love you very much, don't you".

"Yes Doris, I know, and I love you too." That is all she wanted to hear, from then on she was all sweetness and light and a delight to be with.

A BIT DIFFERENT

In spite of the Jekyll and Hyde nature of Colin/Doris I became quite fond of him and was definitely in awe of the talent that exuded from Doris. I booked her for many events and she never failed to grab all the attention with her over the top, comic book looks and cheeky, suggestive manner. She was also good at deflating any false egos that some people endowed themselves with.

Once we took part in an event in a busy shopping centre in Essex, local groups held performances and stalls around the busy square and we had a large stage in the middle, we were having fun. That was until the local Mayor and his cronies turned up, a large car with a flag fluttering from its radiator cap pulled up, the driver scurried around it falling over himself to open the door for his Bumptiousness, the Mayor.

Bedecked with chains and regalia that must have been sponsored by Brasso, he descended from the limo full of pomp and self importance and proceeded to graciously looked upon the participants in a patronising way. Eventually he arrived at our stage and put a 'corporation' smile on his face, Doris's eyes nearly popped out of her head in mock exaltation, she hurried down the steps and tottered up to his Washup and humbly performed the campest curtsy that would have graced any panto scene. Then with a look of admiration on her 'little girl' face grabbed the mayor by the arm, cosied up to him and led him round the square as if besotted by him. Out came the cameras, including the local press, as the hordes of punters laughed out loud. Any pretensions that Mr. Mayor may have had melted in the warmth of Doris's humour and the Mayor, not wanting to be left out of the fun, joined in the camp proceedings, much to the joy of the locals.

When we were performing at the Hackney Show on Hackney Downs, Doris had the opportunity to demonstrate her superior ability to grab the attention of uninterested punters. The whole of the Downs was packed with many tents, marquees, performance areas, a huge music stage and a mighty Fun Fair. We were going down so well in the Variety tent when suddenly all electrical power to the field was cut off. A strange silence fell upon the previously noisy proceedings and within minutes the beer tent became the centre of attraction, all the performers across the whole event stood waiting for something to happen. All of them, that is, except for the irrepressible Doris who was not going to let a technicality get in the way of her sharing her talent with the very fortunate people of Hackney. The huge comical figure of Doris dashed into the beer tent with her flimsy gown flapping in the breeze followed closely by Laurence Payne, causing the tightly packed horde of boozers to step aside as if they knew something special was about to be revealed to them. Laurence sat at the acoustic Joanna and thumped out Doris's trademark saucy songs as our wonderful Doris captivated everyone with her larger than life, naughty performance. The organisers of the Hackney Show were delighted and told me so in no uncertain terms.

Another time when I organised a Talent Contest for a town council in Sussex, I asked Colin to be the celebrity guest on the panel of judges. Well I had asked Colin but Doris arrived and took her place in the panel's rather staid line up, there in the middle of all the besuited and proper dignitaries sat a very large Dame complete with sparkling frock, red rouged cheeks and those spider like eyelashes that fluttered enough to replace the air conditioning system, all this was finished off with a large hat decorated with the biggest ostrich plumes in the south of England. All eyes were on Doris and then she was asked to announce the results of the contest which she did in a gracious and extremely comical way, then, instead of sitting down again, threw herself into 15 minutes of sparkling cabaret that sent the large audience into a frenzy of fun.

Doris was so elated and pleased with me for giving her the gig. and again told me how much she loved me but Colin was back to his normal difficult self. He sat in the van finding fault all the way back to London.

A BIT DIFFERENT

I sometimes felt that all this grumpiness was an act because he could be so kind and thoughtful. After all the shows that we did together I would receive a postcard with a hand written message of thanks on the back of it. A few times he insisted on visiting my mum, who was in a residential home, taking a bunch of flowers and a lot of affection with him. When she died I received another of his postcards with a message of condolence on it, I still have that card.

Doris was born solely to be a pantomime dame and once a year we lost her to Pantoland.

In my opinion she was the best of all the dames. My opinion was shared by the producers who booked her to star with many leading actors in some of the top Pantos. I went to see many of them and can honestly say that although these actors were marvellous they could never hold a candle to Doris (what an image that phrase conjures up) who simply filled the stage with her larger than life saucy personality and talent.

I phoned Colin with the offer of a gig but in his usual snappy way he told me that he was not well and put the phone down, nothing different there then. He resumed work but it was clear that all was not good with him, he had lost a bit of weight but when Doris took over her performance was as strong as ever. The very noble Mickie Driver gave her a lot of work and kept a caring eye on her and she continued to stay at the top of her trade, but we somehow knew that she needed to seek medical help. Of course, she never bothered.

When I booked her for a Steam Festival where we performed in a large marquee she appeared to be the same old Doris, even admiring the fanciable good looks of the client, and gave us a lively and hilarious spot. After the interval she sat in the dressing room, I told her that she was due to do her second spot, she very unusually told me to do her a favour and fill in for her - something she had never done before. It was then that I realised that her illness was more serious than we had thought. Soon after she disappeared from the scene, phone calls were unanswered and messages ignored, so dear old Mickie visited her flat and hammered the door until it was opened, he was shocked by what he saw, they both wept. An ambulance was called and Doris was admitted to hospital, this was the first medical consultation that she had.

    She was diagnosed with cancer and admitted to the esteemed St. Joseph's Hospice in Hackney, where she was visited by her close friends. After a couple of weeks I went, along with Vincent, to say our farewells but on arrival we met Mickie in the foyer, he looked forlorn as he told us that Doris had died. She was just fifty years old.

A BIT OF EAST END HISTORY

The funeral was set for a Saturday morning, an unusual time, quite fitting for such an unusual person. I went accompanied by Jah Globe, a well known reggae artist who was a big fan of Doris's, we knew that the cortege would leave from The Sebright Arms but did not know what else to expect. It was fairly early and the streets were pretty quiet, that was until we turned into Hackney Road, there many small groups of people were making their way towards the pub, it was now clear that a big event was to take place.

The pavement outside the Sebright was packed with a crowd that spilled into the road, they were outside because the very large pub was packed to capacity, me and Globe forced our way to the bar where the benevolent guvnors were dispensing coffee for all the many guests. I looked around for a familiar face and what I saw filled me with wonder, many variety performers, publicans and theatre people mixed with admirers of Doris and I marvelled at the number of old fashioned Nancy Boys that had assembled for this historic event. I thought that they never existed any more but they must have emerged to honour Doris, most of them were respectfully dressed in black but that is where conformity stopped, lots of them adorned themselves with make up, glittering jewellery, flowers and feathers. I found it strangely moving!

The cortege arrived at the pub and a natural silence fell as the hearse and of course the coffin stood outside for the devotees of Doris to say a final farewell, everything was so respectful. More mourners arrived filling the street, the local press turned up and a car load of policemen were sent to marshall the large crowd.

The hearse led the way as the hordes walked solemnly behind, the police, quite sensibly stopped the traffic in Hackney Road as the funeral crossed on its way to the church, St. Peters. At the door the vicar, the Rev. John Weare, a Music Hall fan and friend of Doris's, greeted everyone, the large church was soon filled but still they came, the overflow being shepherded into the aisles, the side chapels and by the altar. It took nearly 20 minutes just to get everyone in. The atmosphere was electric, no-one quite knew what to expect, that is until the overture was played, "There's No Business Like Show Business"! As the coffin entered the music of Bach brought a lull to the proceedings and as Fr. John mounted the pulpit you could have heard a pin drop. Fr. John said that Colin was not much of a believer and to illustrate told a couple of Doris's saucy vicar gags.

From then on the service took on a life of its own and was more like a performance and celebration with songs, stories and tributes. Phil Starr told a hilarious story of how he and Doris did a double act to a packed house of uninterested punters and how Doris, coming to the end of her tether, slammed the piano lid shut and loudly proclaimed "Goodnight!" The congregation laughed but the laughter was quelled when a very emotional Phil choked back a tear and simply said "Goodnight Doris!"

There were more from representatives from theatres and clubs, more songs, plenty of laughs and even more tears. The celebrated entertainer Joan Reagan sang a song and when a recording of Doris was played loud sobs could be heard. At the end, when the coffin was borne out of St. Peter's to a noisy version of Doris's favourite song "Ring them Bells" the entire audience rose to its feet and applauded, cheered, whistled through their fingers and called 'Encore'. This was when the tears flowed most.

Doris would have loved it, I'm not too sure what Colin would have said.

Doris would often say in jest that when she died and the final curtains were drawn that she would like to get a curtain call and come back to take the applause. To this end she phoned the crematorium and asked the woman on the other end of the line if the curtains could be re-opened and the coffin brought back. With a big grin on her face she added "The silly cow slammed the phone down!" I'm note sure of the validity of this story but as Doris's coffin passed out of the church doors I stood waiting for a grand re-appearance. I'm still waiting!

TIME MARCHES ON!

Just as the title suggests the hours are whizzing past, I used to say that I was approaching old age but now I have to admit that I have well and truly arrived at the dreaded time of my life. However, it is alright for me to mention it but don't let me hear you saying it. There are advantages to these tender years and if you give me a day or two I may be able to remember what they are.

I am still waiting for the phone call from Hollywood, it will come I'm sure, and I'm still being as creative as I can be, these tales are proof of this, and I am still desperately trying to hang on to the last vestiges of my cockiness. I am in my 79th year and still going out to entertain the 'old folk', the problem is that I am older than a lot of them and they want me to sing songs made famous by the latest young stars like Elvis Presley and Cliff Richard.

I have had a lot of pleasure and fun from writing my website, from the reactions from the readers of it and from the story telling sessions that evolved from it. These sessions started unintentionally one afternoon when I went with Michael Topping to a club in Essex to entertain some of the older members. As we set up the electric piano Topping realised that a vital bit of the electrical system was missing. "Don't worry" he said "I'll pop along to a shop and get another one". Of course he hadn't taken into consideration that we were out in the wilds. One of the more confident men from the club told him where to get one so Topping asked him to show him the way to this specialist shop, without hesitation the pair of them departed leaving me in front of fifty or more older people who were looking forward to an hours entertainment. They stared at me with that 'go on, amuse us' look upon their faces so I launched into stories from my writings. These stories were about wartime evacuation, shelters and the bombing of London, very interesting, but these ex-Londoners had been through all this themselves, so every tale that I told them was topped by one or the other of them, just who was entertaining who? Certainly my wartime experiences as a small boy seemed insignificant next to these wartime teenagers' stories of being 'bombed out' and other ordeals, but I consoled myself by saying that 'it was all very good experience' and by the fact that when Topping returned and we had a good old knees up and sing song, the seed of story telling had been planted in my mind.

Soon after I was asked to give a talk in Hackney as part of the Clapton Festival, but my confidence had taken a battering making me unsure of what to say. The talk was due to start at 3pm so I rather nervously arrived well before half past two to find that only a couple of old friends from Chats Palace had come to give me support, one of them was The Guvnor, Alan Rossiter, after all these years he was still encouraging me. They were soon joined by my grandson and his mum and we all sat in silence. With five minutes to go the large room resembled an undertakers convention, then a young couple broke the silence by entering rather gently, then out of the blue about 60 people crowded in and sat themselves ready for whatever it was I was going to give them. When I looked at them my nerves jangled again. Help! They were all young and trendy, how was a boring old bugger like me going to captivate them with tales of rationing and blackouts? Well, off I went and from the very start I put my tongue in my cheek and cracked some ancient jokes, I was shocked when they all laughed aloud so I took them on a tour of the joke museum as I told of shelters, air raids and my mum's fiery antics. I was booked to talk for one hour but after 90 minutes I was just getting into my stride when someone threatened to call the Old Bill to stop me. When I reluctantly stopped rabbiting I received a rapturous standing ovation that seemed to go on for ever, I was humbled and thrilled.

Since then I have taken my ramblings to schools, clubs, churches and once to the top of the Old Hackney Tower, all with great success, well ... there was that time when I went all the way to Sussex on a bitter cold day to address some pensioners in a very warm, snug village hall, I reckon that it must have been the heat that caused them all to fall fast asleep.

I am still carrying an even heavier chip on my shoulder and that fire that once blazed within me is still smouldering but as I get older it takes more of an effort to fan it into flames. The love of my life is still making me weak at the knees and I can proudly say that I have never betrayed my working class principles. I have never done anyone a bad turn, never grassed anyone up and never crossed a picket line! My touchy nature has got me into a few, shall we say, differences of opinions and a couple of appearances in front of a magistrate, but I blame my mum for this. It's all her fault!

Up the workers!

Glossary

Translations of East London Words

Oh Gord Blimey	Oh I say Old Chap!
Kate Karney	The Army
Shalom	Welcome
Mazel Tov	Good Luck
Zie Mir Gezunt	Keep Healthy
Booze	Alcoholic Beverage
Gaff	Inferior Dwelling
The Twins	The Kray Brothers
Gear	Illegal contraband
Holy Friar	Liar
Porky Pies	Lies
Tea Leaf	Thief
Old Bill	Gentlemen of the Constabulary
Horrible Shits	Not very nice persons
Pen and Ink	Stink
Flash	Elaborate display
Bull and Cow	Row, noisy argument
Schermozzle	Similar to a Bull and Cow but in Yiddish
Shit	Waste product of the body
Fiddler	Dishonest Person
Squaddies	Soldiers
Mince Pie	An optical organ
Boat race	Face

Beak	Judge
Piss Head	Alcoholic
Tripe Hound	Slovenly Individual
Joanna	Piano Forte
Cymru am byth	Wales Forever
Guvnor	Proprieter of a Public House
Leave it out, mate!	Oh, do try to desist, old chap!